W9-CAW-578

TABLE OF CONTENTS

CHRISTIANS *at* WORK

Examining the intersection *of* calling & career

Barna

Research commissioned by
Abilene Christian University, Abilene, Texas

Research conducted by
Barna Group, Ventura, California

Funding for this research was made possible by the generous support of Abilene Christian University and The Moriah Foundation. Barna Group was solely responsible for data collection, analysis and writing of the report.

PREFACE

Growing up, the local church was always important to my family. The people with whom we worshipped, took communion and served were the center around which our lives revolved. I was baptized and discipled by a specific and beautiful group of people. My experience of God came through the hands and hearts of my local church family. But we also had a sense of membership in the larger Christian community. The health and destiny and effectiveness of the universal "big C" Church always mattered.

In 2016, when my family had the opportunity to partner with Barna Group and Pepperdine University to study leadership in the American Church, it reminded me of those core values of my upbringing. At the time, for *The State of Pastors,* we chose to focus our attention on the men and women who have been called to lead in the church as senior pastors.

That study was groundbreaking, illuminating, encouraging and sobering. We continue to pray that the insights gained will inform the way we think about pastors and their life's calling and affect the way we train, support and follow their leadership.

Still, we never forgot the crucial place of *lay leaders* in the Church. Our experience has led us to a conviction that there is a mostly silent, unrecognized but crucial army of servants who are at the heart of everything good that is happening in the Kingdom of God. They volunteer in ministries and non-profits in their communities. They serve on boards for Christian schools. They teach Bible classes in their churches. They host small groups in their homes. They plan their vacations around mission trips. These men and women are deeply committed to their local church, they carry a vision for the world—and, pivotally, they show

up to work in the marketplace every Monday morning. They have a deeply integrated understanding of how their commitment to follow Jesus informs the whole of life—work, church, family and so on.

When I think of these highly effective disciples, I think of the life of Daniel or Nehemiah. They occupied a crucial, strategic place in the vision of God, but served from something akin

TOD BROWN cofounded Moriah Real Estate Company in 2008 and serves as its chief operating officer. He also cofounded MRI and Petroleum Strategies, Inc. Brown previously served as an executive pastor and currently participates as a member of the preaching team at Golf Course Road Church of Christ in Midland, Texas. He obtained a Bachelor of Science degree, with honors, from Abilene Christian University and is a member of ACU's Board of Trustees. He is a husband to Lee Ann, a father of four and a grandfather of three.

to the marketplace. I am privileged to know many like them today, through my time in business and in ministry. In fact, my father is one of these exceptional individuals: a profoundly successful businessman, a trusted spiritual advisor, an entrepreneur, a visionary ministry leader and an extraordinarily generous philanthropist. He is equally at home in the boardroom, the hospital hallway, a sanctuary or a mission post. He has served as a church elder, a trustee for multiple Christian universities, on the boards of a publicly traded company and a small local ministry that helps at-risk children. He is as impressively influential as he is unfailingly humble. And, as you'll learn in the pages of this report, he is no unicorn—but he is a minority, part of a group of men and women who work, live and serve with faithful passion.

When Barna and Abilene Christian University, my alma mater, came to us with the possibility of continuing our research with a fresh focus on these lay leaders, we were once again honored and excited to be part of it. Our goal is to understand this particular group of mindful, impactful workers. What are the common experiences and backgrounds that shape them? How can the Church recognize, encourage and support them? And how can the local church and the pastors who lead them multiply their numbers?

We have been deeply blessed to be able to serve alongside David Kinnaman and the team at Barna, in partnership with ACU, to produce this substantive report. We trust their collective expertise and commitment to find and understand those who are integrating their faith and their work. As we come to recognize the role and impact of this group, we hope that Jesus' request in Matthew 9:37 will be fulfilled: "Then he said to his disciples, 'The harvest is plentiful but the workers are few. Ask the Lord of the harvest, therefore, to send out workers into his harvest field.'"

TOD BROWN
COO for The Moriah Foundation

INTRODUCTION

Work. When you hear the word, how does it make you feel? Uneasy? Tired? Maybe even ill? (No, that's not a stretch: Research shows that heart attacks occur most often on Monday mornings, and least on Saturdays and during summer vacations in July.)[1]

Why is this activity that consumes the majority of our waking hours—where we define ourselves and live out our identities—so stressful? What does it mean for us as a culture when our work can be hazardous to our well-being?

For years, Barna has been considering how people—particularly those who follow Christ—feel about their work. In short: People are serious about it. In research for the Barna FRAMES series, we learned more than half of adults (53%) say that it's essential to their happiness to have a job where they can make an impact, and that 46 percent of adults feel anxious about making the wrong career choice.

Further, the 2011 book *You Lost Me* touched on the tension Christian Millennials feel between their faith and their work, especially as they seek careers in mainstream arenas of society. In the years since, that tension has only intensified.

We believe the Church has a huge opportunity—a responsibility even, given the profile of the emerging generation—to incorporate deliberate thinking about work into its discipleship and evangelism efforts.

Our culture is already in the midst of a complete revision of the ways we work—an amazing moment when, thanks to technological advancements, workers are both fearing for their jobs and facing unprecedented new opportunities to create the career of their dreams. As Gallup chairman Jim Clifton puts it, "The single most dominant thought on most people's minds is about having a good job."[2] But jobs alone—even good, regular,

The time is ripe for a new imagination, new definitions and a new theology of work

dependable jobs—won't eliminate emotional angst surrounding work. What people really want, Barna's research indicates, is a job that means something, that changes the world, that fulfills and stirs passions. The time is ripe for a new imagination, new definitions and a new theology of work that speaks to who we are and how we are uniquely made. These conversations will happen with or without the Church. Our hope is that Christians will lead the charge in rethinking what work means and what changes we need to make in order for work to lead to our personal and collective flourishing.

That's why Barna has set out on a new initiative focused on vocation. Though in our American vernacular the word "vocation" has become synonymous with "job," it means much more than that. From the Latin word *vocare* meaning "to name or call," a vocation is an assignment given to you by a "caller." As Christians, we believe that our creator God is the one who calls. He made us, knows us and has a good plan for our lives—in other words, a vocation that he calls us to. Your vocation is made up of the special activities that God created you to perform in the world—a fulfillment of his intention and design for you—which will naturally result in service or benefit to the rest of mankind. While that should include your job, or the work you get paid for doing, it certainly is much more than that. As Steve Garber puts it, "Work, yes, but also families, and neighbors, and citizenship, locally and globally—all of this and more is seen as vocation, that to which I am called as a human being, living my life before the face of God."[3]

Vocation is what we are called to do in the world, and understanding it is an essential part of living a fulfilled and meaningful life. It's a basic of Christian discipleship. But even more than that, it's something *every* human heart longs to know—Christ-follower or not. When people wonder *What am I here for?* the Church should be ready to help them find the answer. Yes, beginning with the knowledge of their Savior, but also with an understanding of their purpose, their calling, their vocation—the day-to-day things they were made to do in the world. What could be more helpful?

When people wonder *What am I here for?* the Church should be ready to help them find the answer. What could be more helpful?

True to our mission of "helping Christian leaders understand the times and know what to do," Barna's vocation project aims to provide the Church with a comprehensive and in-depth examination of how people think and feel about calling, purpose, career and the world of work. Through this research and the ensuing resources, we hope to equip Christian leaders to help people live each day with a deep sense of purpose and fulfillment by discovering their vocation and knowing they are doing the work God created them to do.

Christians at Work is the result of our first study in this multi-year initiative. We wanted to start with a look at work and explore how Christians view this essential part of life. Since work is one of the primary places that we discover and define ourselves, relate to others and live out our faith day by day, we wanted to know what's, well, *working*—and what's not—as people approach their calling and career. We took a special interest in those who are thoughtful about what they do and see their work as an opportunity to advance the Kingdom of God. One of our goals was to identify and understand what drives these exemplars so that leaders can better disciple them and motivate others to find more meaningful work as well.

As you'll see in the pages ahead, we discover much to celebrate about Christians in the workplace! Christians are tuned in to the idea of calling, and many feel that their current jobs are well matched with what they perceive as their calling. In addition, Christians who are intentional at work also report being satisfied with their lives overall. It seems there is a positive connection between enthusiasm in one's work and consistency in one's faith. The two go together.

But there are also warning signs all around our workplaces. The majority of Christians still has little sense of calling when it comes to their work, and that is especially true of those who aren't highly engaged with their faith or church. We see some gaps between generations at work and a potential lack of vision for how generations can mentor and support each other. And while there is a great need for spiritual direction surrounding our work lives, there is not an equal emphasis among churches when it comes to providing that direction for men and women as they struggle to build both families and careers. Churches could do a much better job of helping Christians understand how to live out their faith in the workplace—particularly among those who have yet to discover their vocation or integrate faith and work. The opportunity is before us.

This study and the many more to come in Barna's vocation project are our contribution toward the Church's development of a theology of work. So much good work has been done already on the topic of vocation. Our hope is to complement this work with Barna's unique insights as researchers at the intersection of faith and culture. May it be found useful to theologians, practitioners and other Christian leaders who desire to understand the times and know what to do.

BILL DENZEL
Executive Director,
Barna Vocation Project

DAVID KINNAMAN
President, Barna Group

THE MAKING OF *CHRISTIANS AT WORK*

Conception

Barna has a multi-year vision for studying vocation and providing data-driven resources to help people discover and activate their calling. We, alongside our partners at Abilene Christian University, felt it was natural to begin by researching vocation as it is realized through one's paid occupation, with a goal of finding and learning from the employees who experience an overlap of calling and career.

Exemplars interviewed for this study include:

- Sheryl Anderson—television writer
- Dean Batali—film and TV producer
- Tod Bolsinger—vice president, chief of leadership formation at Fuller Seminary
- Mark Cathy—principal program lead, operator support for Chick-fil-A
- Amy Drennan—LMFT, MAICS, executive director of vocation formation at Fuller Seminary
- Woody Faulk—vice president of innovation & new business ventures for Chick-fil-A
- Makoto Fujimura—artist, writer
- Clint Garman—publican, pastor, vice mayor of Santa Paula, CA
- Phil Graves—senior director of corporate development for Patagonia
- Heather Grizzle—founding partner of Causeway Strategies
- Price Harding—partner at CarterBaldwin
- Chris Herschend—vice chairman for Herschend Family Entertainment
- Rob Hudnut—owner of Rob Hudnut Productions
- Rick Ifland—chair of economics & business department, director of Eaton Center for Entrepreneurship and Innovation at Westmont College
- Rev. Larry James—CEO of CitySquare

- Bethany Jenkins—vice president of forums for The Veritas Forum
- Scott Kauffmann—content lead for Praxis
- David Kim—faith & work consultant
- Dr. Pamela Ebstyne King—author, professor at the Thrive Center at Fuller Theological Seminary
- Stephen Kump—CEO & cofounder for Charityvest
- Michaela O'Donnell Long, PhD—senior director of Max De Pree Center for Leadership, owner of Long Winter Media
- Monty L. Lynn—professor of management at Abilene Christian University
- David Martinez—owner of Manny & Burd
- Sheeba Philip—marketing executive for global brands and non-profits
- Matt Rusten—executive director of Made to Flourish
- Andrew Schuman—director of Veritas Labs at The Veritas Forum
- Steve Shackelford—CEO of Redeemer City to City
- Jeff Shinabarger—author, founder of Plywood People
- Darien Sykes—structural engineer, president of Sykes Consulting

Qualitative Interviews

In late 2017 and early 2018, Barna conducted candid interviews with 33 practitioners representing a range of industries and thought leadership on the subject of faith and work. Researchers used a flexible script exploring respondents' experiences of calling and career. (You can read some of the responses throughout this report in the "Conversations with Practitioners" feature.)

Quantitative Surveys

In early 2018, armed with insights from the qualitative discussions, Barna conducted online quantitative surveys of employed U.S. Christians who agree at least somewhat that their faith is important in their lives today.[*] To get a full picture of how vocation is approached in the Church, a separate study surveyed pastors about their own experiences with and ideas about calling.

Identifying Vocational Personalities

After data was collected, Barna's researchers created a custom segmentation to group respondents by their intention toward and experience of integrating faith and work. Using a cluster analysis based on four chosen measures of fulfillment of one's calling (see page 50), Barna defined and assessed three types of workers: faith-work Integrators, Onlookers and Compartmentalizers.

Areas of Future Inquiry

What kind of vocational satisfaction is reported by those who don't have a paid job, such as stay-at-home parents or retirees?[**] How do the experiences of ethnic minorities or those facing workplace bias affect career sentiments? Which resources or strategies are proving effective in mentoring the tech-savvy, career-oriented next generation of Christian workers? Barna sees these and other questions as opportunities for further research building upon the findings explored in the following pages.

[*] This group is representative of the national population of employed Christians, yet all research that seeks to capture the dynamics of a population has some inherent limitations. For a detailed profile of the study's participants, see the Methodology section.

[**] Findings in this study and other Barna research suggest work-life tension for working mothers in particular. However, this study does not represent men or women who have left the workforce, temporarily or permanently, as a comparison.

KEY FINDINGS: AT A GLANCE

Most Christian workers don't see a strict spiritual hierarchy of professions or a divide between "sacred" and "secular" jobs.

Two-thirds agree on some level that it's clear to them how their own work serves God.

Christian workers seek (and often find) meaningful, purposeful employment

Six in 10 believe they have God-given gifts, and one in three wants a better understanding of them.

... especially if they attend church regularly.

Practicing faith is consistently correlated with feeling well suited to one's work and wanting to have an impact.

For faith-work Integrators, high expectations accompany high satisfaction.

Barna identifies a special group for whom professional curiosity, generosity, integrity and gratification are a package deal.

However, the majority of Christians could use more urgency or certainty in their vocational pursuits.

72 percent are defined as Compartmentalizers or Onlookers when it comes to their calling and career, and only 28 percent qualify as Integrators.

Christian men and women have similar experiences of calling and career—just not at the same time.

While working fathers and single women thrive, working mothers and single men struggle for vocational fulfillment by comparison.

The generational ends of the labor force naturally have different career needs.

Millennials could use some spiritual direction to anchor their ambition, as Boomers' attention transitions from career.

Only half of churched adults feel their church supports them in their career

53 percent say their church helps them understand how to live out their faith in the workplace.

... though not all groups also serve the Church in return.

Job commitments are a hindrance to church involvement, especially for those who approach their work with great spiritual intention.

Pastors appear well-positioned to be vocational leaders and mentors.

The majority is content in their career, mentors others and thinks about how their church can equip workers.

1

A FRESH LOOK AT CALLING & CAREER

"The first step in developing a theology of work must be to study the present reality of human work." —Miroslav Volf

"How do I find meaning in my work?"

It's not a novel question; you've likely asked it yourself. Barna research shows that three-quarters of adults (75%) are looking for ways to live a more meaningful life. If much of that life is spent at work—some have estimated that the average worker will spend 90,000 hours on the clock[4]—it's no surprise Americans want their job to produce passion (39%), even more so than needs such as financial security (33%).

For working Christians, this question of finding meaning could perhaps be rephrased to an even more pointed one: "How do I integrate my faith and my work?" Or, as the apostle Paul asked, "How do I take my everyday, ordinary life—my sleeping, eating, going-to-work and walking-around life—and place it before God as an offering?" (Romans 12:1–2, *The Message*).

It's a largely internal, spiritual intention, but it is manifested externally in a complex professional context. Today, there is no shortage of gray areas to navigate in the workplace. Office hours and leisure time are often indiscernible. Demographic shifts, changing gender dynamics and generational differences require us to rethink the climates and concerns of our workplaces. The same technological advancements that make teams more

effective or connected also tend to create interactions that are isolated or impersonal. And as faithful employees strive to discern purpose and do good in the marketplace, their sincerity might be challenged in a society reluctant to place parameters on truth.

These are just some of the obstacles to vocation as experienced through one's occupation, and it's a subject Barna has been circling for some time. Over the years and multiple projects, our researchers have examined work-life balance in a success-centric culture, assessed what prospective students ultimately want from Christian higher education and studied pastors' ministry callings. We've asked employed adults about the minutiae of their daily routines, experiences of workplace inequality or injustice, expectations for retirement and even their involvement in office romances. We've particularly had the microscope on Millennials, a job-hopping group whose professional ambitions are rivaled only by their professional anxieties. Now, as Millennials dominate the workforce and we turn our sights to Gen Z, we've learned that today's teens are perhaps more oriented around academic and professional success—and less defined by Christian faith—than any other adult generation Barna has observed.

The professional and spiritual stakes are high. A failure to provide vocational discipleship could be a failure to help Christians, especially younger ones, keep their faith.[5] So the goal of this report—which examines a sample of employed, self-identified Christians in the United States who agree at least somewhat that their faith is important to them—is to offer a far-reaching, deeply introspective assessment of a sense of vocation in the Church, specifically through one's profession (as distinct from other valuable yet unpaid forms of vocation, like volunteering, hobbies, parenting, homemaking, etc.).

As the world and our workplaces rapidly

LET'S TALK ABOUT ... WHAT "CALLING" MEANS

" I believe vocation and thriving occur at the intersection of self, other and Christ. In other words, vocation not only involves being strength-based and living out of one's passions and propensities while building God's Kingdom here on earth, but also being conformed to the image of God in Christ."

—Dr. Pamela Ebstyne King, author, professor at the Thrive Center at Fuller Theological Seminary

change—each uniquely marked by trends of digitization, globalization, secularization and individualization—it's never been more important for people of faith to think deeply about what they are made to do and why they do it. We have reason to believe it's already on their mind: Five years ago, one-third of employed Christians (34%) had never even thought about whether they felt "called" to their work. Today, that percentage has dropped to 15.

We'll begin here—with the encouraging finding that many Christian workers in the U.S. are at least in tune with a sense of calling, if not experiencing a healthy, even rewarding, relationship with their work.

CHRISTIANS AT WORK: AN OVERVIEW

Six in 10 working Christian adults believe they've been given certain skills and talents to use for God's glory (61%) or for the good of others (61%). Granted, not all of these Christians know what these gifts might be or how they should be applied—four in 10 (40%) agree strongly that they are aware of them, and one in three (34%) wants to know more about how they could serve God through these talents.

Even though all of the Christians Barna surveyed see their faith as valuable, there are some consistent gaps along theolographic lines.[6] Specifically, we found discrepancies between believers with a practicing faith and those who are more on the fringes of the Church. We will explore this further—but it is evident that participation in a faith community has a positive correlation

> A failure to provide vocational discipleship could be a failure to help Christians keep their faith

> 66 Calling means the responsibility and purpose that I have in life, and the action that coincides with that. ... It can take different paths, at different seasons of life."
>
> —Jeff Shinabarger, author, founder of Plywood People

> 66 It's that alignment of what God is doing in the world and your surroundings, and its overlap with your giftings and your abilities. ... It's the engine of your entire life."
>
> —Sheeba Philip, marketing executive for global brands and non-profits

Conversations with Practitioners

Practicing faith consistently and clearly surfaces as important for thriving in one's vocation

with one's experiences and beliefs about faith and work integration. Overall, practicing Christians (defined by Barna as those who *strongly* agree their faith is important to them and attend church at least monthly) have more clarity in this regard. For example, this group, which makes up 43 percent of the sample, are 36 percentage points more likely than their non-practicing peers (81% vs. 45%) to strongly affirm that they possess God-given gifts, and more than half (52% vs. 31%) are acutely aware of said gifts. Here and throughout the survey, practicing faith consistently and clearly surfaces as important for thriving in one's vocation.

Many Christians feel their current employment is also well-matched with their sense of calling. Three-quarters are at least somewhat satisfied with this measure of their career (39% "very," 36% "somewhat"). A majority of Christian workers says that their unique strengths, talents and abilities are being utilized in their present job (42% "strongly" agree, 43% "somewhat" agree). Just over a quarter (26% "strongly" agree) sees how their job description serves God or a higher purpose, up slightly from 20 percent when Barna asked this question in 2014. Predictably, we see all of these trends amplified when comparing practicing and non-practicing Christians; among the latter, just 15 percent clearly recognize how their work might serve God.

Awareness of Personal Gifts and Talents
% agree strongly

◆ All Christians   ◆ Non-practicing Christians   ◆ Practicing Christians

I believe God gave me certain gifts and talents to use for his glory — 61% / 45% / 81%

I want to use my gifts and talents for the good of others — 61% / 52% / 73%

I am aware of the gifts and talents God has given me — 40% / 31% / 52%

I wish I had a clearer understanding of how I should use my gifts and talents to serve God — 34% / 32% / 36%

n=1,459 employed U.S. Christians.

How Christians Feel About Their Current Work

◆ All Christians   ◆ Non-practicing Christians   ◆ Practicing Christians

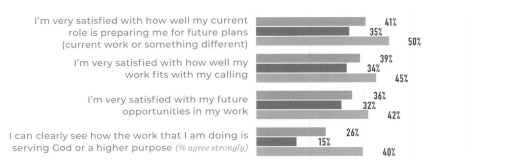

I'm very satisfied with how well my current role is preparing me for future plans (current work or something different)
41%
35%
50%

I'm very satisfied with how well my work fits with my calling
39%
34%
45%

I'm very satisfied with my future opportunities in my work
36%
32%
42%

I can clearly see how the work that I am doing is serving God or a higher purpose *(% agree strongly)*
26%
15%
40%

n=1,459 employed U.S. Christians.

Where Working Christians Apply Their Gifts

42%

My work utilizes my unique strengths, talents and capabilities
(% agree strongly)

29%

I find ways to use my unique strengths, talents and capabilities outside the workplace
(% "very true")

n=1,459 employed U.S. Christians.

Overall, Christians are mostly contented in their employment: More than three-quarters of Christians in the workforce are either very (35%) or somewhat (39%) satisfied with their current job. Just 5 percent report being very unsatisfied. For all indicators of satisfaction, practicing Christians outpace their non-practicing peers in consistently feeling suited for and fulfilled by their work. Barna's survey does not include the general U.S. population, but for comparison, a Conference Board study finds half of all U.S.

Overall Job Satisfaction Is High

Taking all factors into account, how satisfied or unsatisfied are you overall with your current job?

◆ Very satisfied ◆ Somewhat satisfied ◆ Neutral ◆ Somewhat unsatisfied ◆ Very unsatisfied

Practicing Christian workers

All Christian workers

n=1,459 employed U.S. Christians.

workers today are satisfied in their jobs,[7] and Gallup's 12-point assessment deems a third of the American workforce "engaged."[8]

When it comes to identifying what most matters to them in employment, Christians' primary concerns are both personal and financial: Two-thirds want a job that provides a sense of purpose (65% "very" important) and competitive pay and benefits (68%). Half look for flexibility in their working arrangements (50%) or opportunities for advancement (50%). With the latter in mind, it's a good sign that a majority of Christian workers also believes that their current work opens up doors for their future plans (76% "somewhat" + "very" satisfied) or for future opportunities at work (72% "somewhat" + "very" satisfied). Forty-two percent of Christians highly prioritize working for the greater good of society and the world.

Beyond these preferences, it may not matter to most Christians whether they or someone else works in a "sacred" or "secular" space. Barna asked whether it was better for a Christian to become a pastor or missionary, or to represent his or her faith well at work. In general, Christians are most likely to say that neither one is superior to the other (64%). After all, almost two-thirds of employed Christians (64%) agree on some level that it's clear to them how their work serves God or a higher purpose. This indicates that Christians are prone to see spiritual value in any working context—or that

Two-thirds of employed Christians agree on some level that it's clear to them how their work serves God or a higher purpose perhaps the marketplace seems to them as urgent a mission field as any. Though, as explored in the infographic on page 30, they most often associate religious and pastoral roles with being a calling or serving the common good.

Top Employment Priorities Split Between Purposeful and Practical

How important are each of the following when it comes to finding or staying in a particular job?

◆ Very important ◆ Somewhat important ◆ Not too important ◆ Not at all important

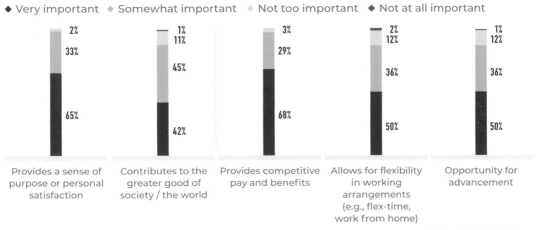

Provides a sense of purpose or personal satisfaction	Contributes to the greater good of society / the world	Provides competitive pay and benefits	Allows for flexibility in working arrangements (e.g., flex-time, work from home)	Opportunity for advancement

n=1,459 employed U.S. Christians.

Ministry Is Not Seen as Superior to Other Work

Do you personally think it is better for a Christian to become a pastor or missionary, or to represent their faith well in their place of work?

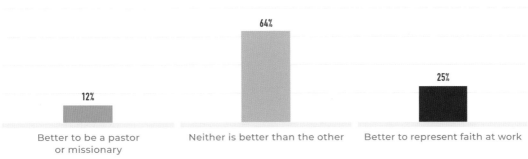

Better to be a pastor or missionary	Neither is better than the other	Better to represent faith at work
12%	64%	25%

n=1,459 employed U.S. Christians.

Types of Employment

In this sample of Christian workers, a large majority (73%) is employed full-time, while almost one in five (17%) is employed part-time. Ten percent are self-employed. The top industries represented are health science and medical technology; education; child development and family services; manufacturing and product development; and finance and business. Nearly a third, however, falls into an industry that was not listed.

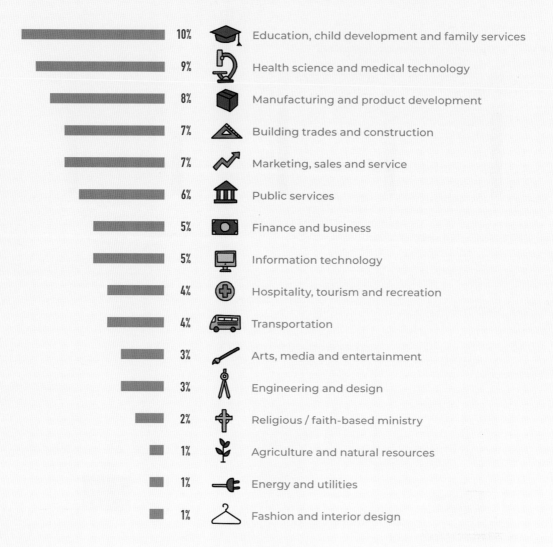

10%		Education, child development and family services
9%		Health science and medical technology
8%		Manufacturing and product development
7%		Building trades and construction
7%		Marketing, sales and service
6%		Public services
5%		Finance and business
5%		Information technology
4%		Hospitality, tourism and recreation
4%		Transportation
3%		Arts, media and entertainment
3%		Engineering and design
2%		Religious / faith-based ministry
1%		Agriculture and natural resources
1%		Energy and utilities
1%		Fashion and interior design

n=1,459 employed U.S. Christians. Thirty-one percent of respondents fell into the "other, not listed" category.

GENERATIONAL IDEAS OF VOCATION VARY

The Great Recession of the late 2000s likely looms over many current mindsets about career. Though the economy has recovered in some ways, the working lives of many Gen X and Boomers have been marked by spells of unemployment or persistent debt,[9] and the leading edge of Boomers is just now cozying up to the idea of retirement.[10] Millennials, meanwhile, entered a fairly unwelcoming job market at the very beginning of their careers.

It's not too surprising, then, that Barna sees occasional differences in how generations consider vocation via work, whether because of their season in life or because of the unique economic and professional climates in which they are building, or have built, their careers. (The Elder and Gen Z segments are relatively small and not included for analysis here,

due in part to their lower participation in the workforce.) Similar proportions of all working Christians, regardless of age, believe God gave them specific talents intended for his glory. From there, however, feelings surrounding vocation become more mixed, particularly when looking at the generational bookends of the labor force: Boomers and Millennials.

Christian Millennial workers appear to be finding a place for themselves and their capabilities in the workforce—half (50%) strongly agree they feel made for the work they currently do—and they are hopeful about their future prospects. This optimism doesn't necessarily stem from great success; low earnings still dog Millennials, even as general wages have caught up to pre-recession levels.[11] So if they aren't *earning* more green, is it just

A Sense of Vocation, by Generation
% agree strongly

◆ Millennials ◆ Gen X ◆ Boomers

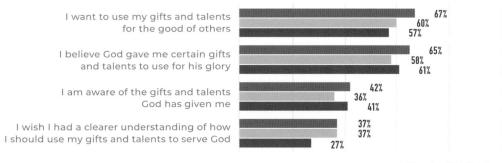

n=1,459 employed U.S. Christians.

"I find ways to use my unique strengths, talents and capabilities outside the workplace"

◆ Very true   ◆ Somewhat true   ◆ Somewhat untrue   ◆ Very untrue

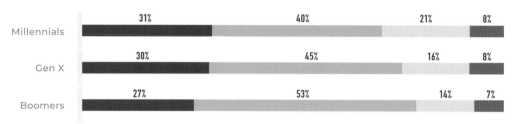

n=1,403 employed U.S. Christians.

that working Millennials *are* green? Certainly, much has been written (and bemoaned) about Millennial idealism. Barna's research at least suggests that the Christians in the largest generation in the modern labor force[12] are buoyed in these formative working years both by a deep sense of ambition and by the hope of making a difference. Millennials tend to be very conscious of their talents (42%) as well as hopeful for a better understanding of

them (37%). They are also motivated to be generous with their unique skills; more than two-thirds (67%) report that they hope to use them in service of others, 10 percentage points more than the proportion of Boomers motivated by this idea.

Boomers have less of a sense that they are "made for" their present work (39%) and they feel less urgency to deepen an understanding of their gifts (27%), but we shouldn't assume

LET'S TALK ABOUT ... HOW TO FIND YOUR CALLING

❝ How do people discover their callings? Interrogating your opportunities, your passions and the things that seem to get a lot of approval and fruit, combined with things that you seem to individually be obsessed and passionate about and with the opportunities God gives you."

—*Scott Kauffmann, content lead for Praxis*

❝ I would challenge [young people] to ask themselves, when somebody is reading their eulogy about you, what is it that you want them to say? Then, work backwards from there. See the end now and work backwards."

—*Darien M. Sykes, structural engineer, president of Sykes Consulting*

Professional Fulfillment, by Generation

◆ Millennials   ◆ Gen X   ◆ Boomers

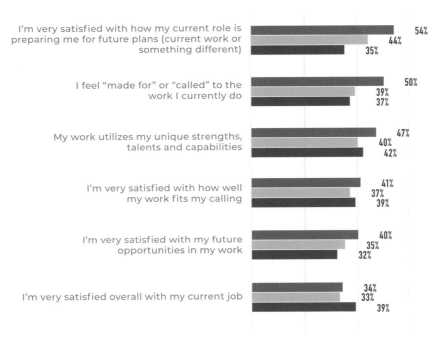

I'm very satisfied with how my current role is preparing me for future plans (current work or something different)
54%
44%
35%

I feel "made for" or "called" to the work I currently do
50%
39%
37%

My work utilizes my unique strengths, talents and capabilities
47%
40%
42%

I'm very satisfied with how well my work fits my calling
41%
37%
39%

I'm very satisfied with my future opportunities in my work
40%
35%
32%

I'm very satisfied overall with my current job
34%
33%
39%

n≈1,403 employed U.S. Christians.

> 66 I like to think of it as layers. I feel very called to create. I feel very called to learn, usually through my own research. I feel very called to teach. But I've now come to expect, especially as I've understood more about how the economy works and the way structures are shifting, that those things take very different shapes based on seasons in my life. I think calling is something that is both crystal clear and incredibly muddy."
>
> —*Michaela O'Donnell Long, PhD, senior director of Max De Pree Center for Leadership, owner of Long Winter Media*

Conversations with Practitioners

Christian Millennial workers appear to be finding a place for themselves and their capabilities in the workforce

that means they aren't attuned to or using them. Sure, they express less enthusiasm about future opportunities, but that may be because they feel more presently secure, having already climbed (or grown skeptical of) the corporate ladder. And given that Boomers often tell Barna their identity is defined by family, we may simply be witnessing a natural shift in life priorities that comes with age. In other words, Millennials might expect more of their professional future because there is more of it, while Boomers are in a less exploratory, even stable, season of career. Regardless, they are similarly satisfied in their current work, and Boomers find purposes for their unique skills *outside* the office too (80% vs. 71% of Millennials say this is "very" + "somewhat" true), which bodes well for their golden years.

LET'S TALK ABOUT ... HOW TO FIND YOUR CALLING

" Can you go create your calling, or do you wait on your calling? I think the answer is both. With all intent, you do an assessment of your unique wiring, and your gifts, and your talents, and your passions and your interests in light of your dream."

—*Woody Faulk, vice president of innovation & new ventures for Chick-fil-A*

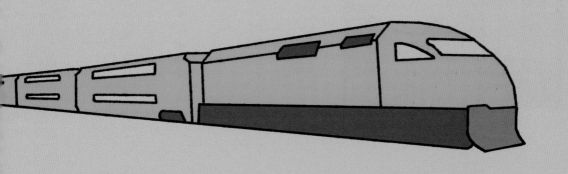

GOOD WORK

**"CALLING" IS FIRST ASSOCIATED WITH
MINISTERING TO OR SERVING OTHERS.**
The majority of Christian workers sees potential for a variety of occupations to be categorized as "callings." But there is a subtle perceived hierarchy in this regard, with ministry-related jobs at the top and more technical jobs at the bottom.

A CALLING MAY NOT BE LIMITED TO THE OFFICE.
As a comparison, Barna also asked whether respondents see an inherent calling in one common yet unpaid task: raising kids. Parenthood does rank highly, just behind pastoral roles, indicating Christians also understand calling in a broad sense—as something fulfilled within and beyond a profession.

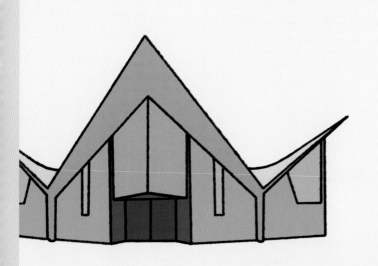

Usually a calling	Sometimes a calling		
69%	13%	1.	Pastor
67%	17%	2.	Missionary
59%	25%	3.	Worship leader
52%	35%	4.	Parent
44%	40%	5.	Church staff, other than pastor
37%	40%	6.	Firefighter
36%	42%	7.	Pediatrician
32%	45%	8.	Musician
30%	42%	9.	Military officer
25%	42%	10.	Athlete
20%	38%	11.	Plastic surgeon
11%	46%	12.	Financial advisor
11%	45%	13.	Accountant
6%	32%	14.	School janitor

Which jobs do Christians consider to be "callings?"

◆ Usually a calling ◆ Sometimes a calling

Pastor — 1.
Missionary — 2.
Worship leader — 3.
Parent — 4.
Church staff, other than pastor — 5.
Firefighter — 6.
Pediatrician — 7.
Musician — 8.
Military officer — 9.
Athlete — 10.
Plastic surgeon — 11.
Financial advisor — 12.
Accountant — 13.
School janitor — 14.

80%
60%
40%
20%

n=1,459 employed U.S. Christians.

THE MYTH OF "SACRED VS. SECULAR" JOBS

Redemptive work is not exclusive to one title or industry

BY CORY MAXWELL-COGHLAN

The command of Genesis 1:28 to "be fruitful and multiply" and to "rule over every living thing" is a call to cultivate the earth and exercise dominion. This is often referred to as the cultural mandate. God deliberately created the world with a capacity for development and we, as his image-bearers, are to continue this ever-unfolding work by building and sustaining culture. And in his providence, God remains involved, directing this work as the great superintendent. But, as Al Wolters points out in his book *Creation Regained,* if we are tempted to see the work that leads to the building of institutions—as well as the general unfolding of human history and culture—as alien to God's purposes in the world, then it's easy to brand them as inherently "secular."[13]

When asked whether it's better for Christians to become pastors or missionaries or to represent their faith well in their place of work, almost two-thirds (64%) say neither is better than the other. However, when asked which professions have the most potential to serve the common good or to be considered a calling, there is a clear preference for "religious leader" and "missionary." This preference is often the result of a two-realm theory, where one is considered *sacred* and the other *secular.* This false distinction is often referred to as dualism, and it comes from a misunderstanding of the operation of grace, and the categories of creation, fall and redemption.

When we consider some professions as "secular" and others as "sacred," we risk saying God's hand is absent from some professions. But if we're able to see that the culture-building commanded of us in the original mandate is part of the blueprint for God's masterpiece, then it becomes possible to serve God

---

"When we conflate God's Kingdom with the institutional Church, we restrict the scope of God's work and kingship."

---

in industries like business, politics, media and technology.[14] Even janitors and accountants serve the common good. When we conflate God's Kingdom with the institutional Church (i.e., only clergy or missionaries are engaging in full-time sacred work) we restrict the scope of God's work and kingship.[15]

The temptation to categorize creation into these two realms also comes from a misunderstanding of the pervasiveness of both sin and redemption. The whole of creation is affected by the fall, but the good news is that the whole of creation is also *reclaimed* in Christ.[16] Colossians 1:20 says Christ is determined to "reconcile to himself *all* things." This means that *all* creation is included in the scope of his redemptive work. In his book *Every Good Endeavor*, Timothy Keller argues that "people with this view cannot see that work done by non-Christians always contains some degree of God's common grace as well as the distortions of sin. And they cannot see that work done by Christians, even if it overtly names the name of Jesus, is also significantly distorted by sin."[17] If we go to work believing that Christ's redemptive reach has not made it to our desk, then we end up "excluding certain areas of our lives from the *need* for reform."[18] But this fails to grasp the full reach of God's Kingdom and redemption. Being a Christian means believing that God is at work in the *whole* of our lives, that the gospel reframes everything, not just the overtly religious things.[19]

We ought to not only engage our faith at work, but also engage the culture—including all the "secular" parts—with our faith.[20] This opens our eyes to a new world of recognizing all kinds of beauty and goodness in the world, appreciating not only the hand of God behind the work of our colleagues and neighbors,[21] but believing this even for our own work outside the church. ◢

CORY MAXWELL-COGHLAN is a senior writer at Barna Group. He has a master's degree in religion & politics from Harvard University and a background in ministry, entrepreneurship and the non-profit sector. Hailing from Australia, he currently lives in New York City.

THE FAMILY FACTOR

Vocational parity between men and women exists —just not in every stage of life

Through the lens of this survey—focused on the overlap of calling and career—vocational fulfillment appears widespread, even where broader occupational inequality may exist.[22] In several crucial ways, Christian men and women in this study share goals and qualities as collaborators in work and the Kingdom. They are similarly likely to feel "called" in their line of work (42% of working men vs. 40% of working women) or to strongly agree that their job serves God or a higher purpose (27% vs. 24%). They want to make a difference in the world. They seek to learn and improve themselves. They find purpose and feel their strengths are put to use, inside and outside the workplace. For the most part, their professional and financial priorities are in sync.

Christian men, however, have a slight edge when it comes to feeling optimistic about their professional futures, embracing risk or identifying as entrepreneurial. Yet Christian women are bold on other measures, like aiming to impart grace and peace to others in their work (53% vs. 44%). This echoes other research that confirms the American public looks to women for leadership that is compassionate, organized or honest, while men's leadership style is seen as more decisive and driven.[23] Fittingly, "relational / emotional support" is the most common form of generosity that Christian women tell Barna they offer to others (47% vs. 32%).

Though both men and women feel a vocational connection with their churches, women don't seem to have as much energy to give back. Female church attendees are less likely to be using their work-related gifts to serve the Church (32% vs. 43% of men who attend church monthly), and roughly one-third (31% vs. 18%) says being too tired hinders their involvement.

The point at which these gender gaps grow stark is when parenting enters the picture. Society has long debated whether women can "have it all"—or what that means in the first place.[24] This study suggests that women are making more compromises than men do in pursuit of a family and / or a satisfying career.

Based on this study alone, Barna can't weigh in on how vocation is experienced among stay-at-home-parents, as the sample was made up of only employed Christians, and the aim was to specifically explore vocational attitudes within one's paid occupation.

But as U.S. women increasingly assume the role of sole or at least cobreadwinner, these findings have widespread implications in both the home and workplace.[25] We know from other research that about half of unmarried U.S. adults (53%) say they would like to marry,[26] and 9 in 10 U.S. adults want children.[27] Even if at lower rates than in the past, the majority of U.S. adults will marry at some point,[28] and we can likely assume that most of the single Christians in this sample are on a path toward marriage and family. Further, a Barna study in 2015 showed most women (53% vs. 30% of men) don't believe someone should have to put off having children until after establishing a career. (No wonder flexibility is one of the few characteristics that women are more likely than men to see as very important in a job.)

A lack of support or outlets for mothers' gifts within or beyond the workplace thus seems to be a vocational roadblock for working women—even though parenthood is

Attitudes Toward Vocation, by Relationship / Family Status

◆ Single men   ◆ Single women   ◆ Fathers   ◆ Mothers

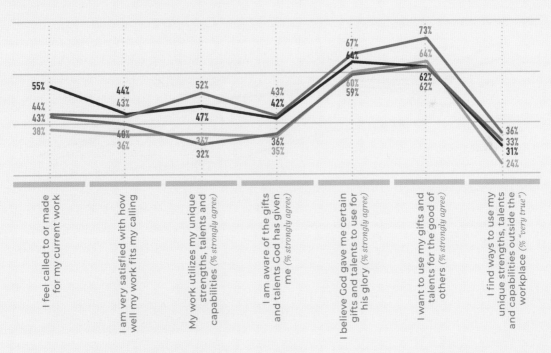

n=765 employed U.S. Christians.

35

widely regarded as a calling on its own (see page 30). While working mothers are relatively gratified in their family relationships, Barna sees they are well behind on all metrics of satisfaction—relational, spiritual, emotional, you name it. On top of this, mothers in the working world face a number of financial blows; as the *Washington Post* quips, "America's gender wage gap is more of a *maternal* wage gap."[29] At the same time that mothers may find

themselves struggling to advance in their career, fathers who desire greater participation in caregiving or homemaking might feel entrenched in the workforce and unable to share the weight of emotional labor.[30]

Mostly, however, there is no clear tradeoff between Christian fathers' work satisfaction and satisfaction in other areas of life: They are pleased with their future professional prospects, as well as their relationships, quality of

Vocational Values, by Relationship / Family Status

As a Christian in my workplace, I believe it is "completely" important to...

◆ Single men   ◆ Single women   ◆ Fathers   ◆ Mothers

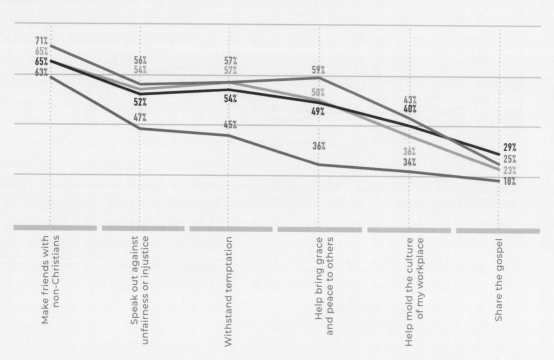

n=765 employed U.S. Christians.

life, spiritual well-being and emotional and mental health. That doesn't mean there aren't growing pains for fathers figuring out work-life balance: In Barna research for the book *The Tech-Wise Family*, men were twice as likely as women (20% vs. 10%) to say that the demands of the daily grind made parenting difficult, and more often expressed that their kids wished they didn't work so much while at home (26% vs. 18% strongly agree). But working fathers' broader optimism and perceived validation of their God-given talents reflect other established trends in U.S. society, such as the professional boost new dads experience[31] and the "motherhood penalty" awaiting many new moms.[32]

Tellingly, the sweet spot for Christian women's vocational fulfillment is actually when they have never even been married. This segment of women is more likely to prioritize

Career Support from Church, by Relationship / Family Status

◆ Single men   ◆ Single women   ◆ Fathers   ◆ Mothers

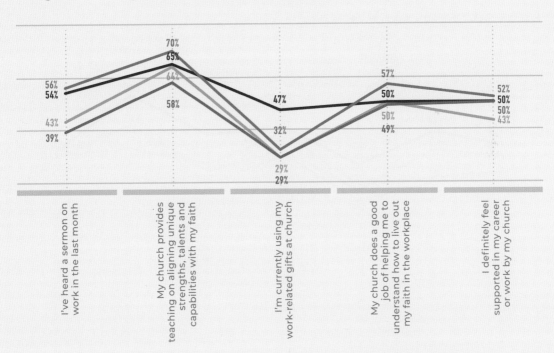

n=395 employed U.S. Christians who attend church monthly.

embodying spiritual and relational strengths in work, and they find a drive and gratification exceeding even that of working fathers. Though they still aren't especially involved in serving their churches, these never-married women feel vocationally supported by the Church, and nearly three-quarters (73%) hope to use their gifts for the good of others.

Single women's mostly well-rounded well-being is even more remarkable compared to their single male peers: Never-married Christian men are least attuned to, supported in or satisfied by their vocation and exhibit a somewhat alarming lack of spiritual thinking about their work. As single women go about integrating their faith and work, single men appear surprisingly unengaged by comparison.

This survey can't draw conclusions about the causes or effects of these patterns among men and women. Certainly, each Christian and each family is shaped by individual temperaments, financial contexts, seasons of life,

Satisfaction Levels, by Relationship / Family Status
% very satisfied

◆ Single men　◆ Single women　◆ Fathers　◆ Mothers

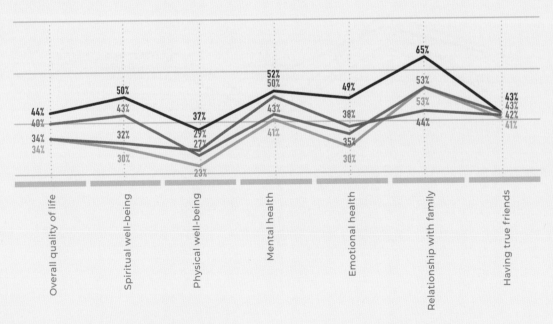

n=765 employed U.S. Christians.

generational priorities and spiritual convictions that inform a man or woman's function within and beyond the home. And as younger adults continue to postpone or forego getting married or having kids in favor of career building, who knows how these trends may continue to evolve?[33] But it does seem clear that churches are missing chances to speak to or anticipate the modern-day vocational needs of congregants, whether they are single, married or rearing children.

How can faith communities create environments that rally around the realities of working adults today? And what might our homes, churches and workplaces have to gain when both men and women are able to identify and apply their God-given gifts—at every stage of life and career?

LIFE AS MINISTRY

A Q&A with Jo Saxton

Q What does "calling" mean to you?

A I've often found it easier to look back and recognize calling, rather than to see it as a blueprint for how to live life. I think there are broad brushstrokes, which are vague enough for everyone: to know God well and to represent him in the world.

I would encourage people who are wondering about their calling to look at some practical things. First, look at the life you already have: Where's your job? Who are the people you are interacting with regularly? What would it look like to represent God there? How does it affect you being a neighbor, a friend, a customer, a consumer?

Then I would ask, what are you good at? Maybe you've got a great way with numbers, or with hospitality or with organizing people. How have those things been employed in the past? And are they being employed in the present?

Finally, what needs to be done? If God is making all things new, and we see old things that are damaging people, then we've got a part to play in that through our lives, our language, our prayers and our relationships. I would ask, do you have a particular passion in

"The things that make us angry, make us cry or get us agitated are often the things God may be nudging us toward."

the overarching scheme of representing God in the world? Are you always drawn to a particular community, network of relationships or type of people? The things that make us angry, make us cry or get us agitated are often the things God may be nudging us toward, to represent him in those places.

Q What do you think accounts for some of the gender gaps we see in vocational experiences? How can churches equip both men and women to thrive in their vocation, regardless of what that might look like?

A First of all, if we're helping women integrate faith and work, whether she is a stay-at-home mom or is holding down a career, articulate to those women that they are both representing God in the world.

But in our current age, more and more women are at work, and staying at home is actually more often a privilege or economic freedom. It's not even about vocation; it's about bills. Sometimes the Church is talking to a world which only exists for a limited few, and that can leave feelings of guilt and uncertainty for the rest. I've talked with a lot of women who are working out how they can pursue their passion, and they often ask whether they have permission to do that, because it feels somehow like betrayal to work and to love it.

For mothers, the issues of fulfillment and vocation become conflicting. There are choices that are made at certain intersections of a woman's life, and the pathway is not as linear as a man's often is. When you have both partners working, the woman is still often carrying the load of the domestic tasks, arranging the family's and child's schedules. Who is staying home if somebody's got strep throat? I've heard it described as the "mental load," and that's a job on top of another job. I think it's like having too many tabs open on your laptop; everything slows down. Fundamental things like maternity leave or childcare have a massive impact.

Q Some groups, like the Compartmentalizers mentioned in this report (see page 50), might feel like work is just something they must do, or wonder why it is even important to feel placed or fulfilled in work. What would you say to them about the sacred nature of all work?

A I think they raise valid points, because it is a bit of luxury to get wistful about work. In my first job as a cleaner, I don't know that I found any joy in it at all; it just paid bills. And for some of us, the greater purpose of vocation

JO SAXTON
Pastor, author, leadership coach

Born to Nigerian parents and raised in London, Saxton is an author, speaker, leadership coach and church planter who brings a multicultural, international perspective to leadership. She has served on staff in multiple churches in the United Kingdom and the United States. Currently, she is chair of the board for 3DM, a non-profit organization that equips churches in discipleship and mission, and serves on the advisory board for *Today's Christian Woman*. Saxton's books include *More Than Enchanting, High Heels and Holiness* and *The Dream of You,* and she cohosts the podcast *Lead Stories: Tales of Leadership in Life*. She and her husband, Chris, live in Minneapolis with their two daughters.

is in the fact that it means you can provide for your family and provide for opportunities. I think that's just being honest.

But as a Church, in our explicit and implicit communication, we've made mission something that happens "over there" rather than at a cubicle. We don't publicly celebrate the daily grind of working in a job, because it's not particularly glamorous. We forget to tell people that our heroes of faith had jobs. Deborah really was a judge. Daniel really worked in government. Luke really was a doctor. Paul really did make tents. Lydia really was a businesswoman. We've forgotten to contextualize and apply that reality. These are people who had opportunities for Kingdom engagement.

Because we are in relationship with God, we also represent him in the world. No, it may not be in a sermon, but I think life is a ministry. We have this one gift of a life, and many hours of it are spent in our workplace. What does it look like to partner with God and what he's doing in the world in your workplace? ◪

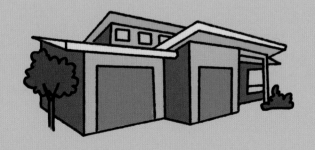

ALL IN A LIFE'S WORK

Each age or stage corresponds with different dreams and needs in one's career. Christian Millennials, the least financially stable, are in a season of exploration and independence (indeed, half remain unmarried).

Making a difference

67% of Millennials want to use their gifts and talents for the good of others

58% of Millennials want to make a difference in the world

58% of Millennials believe it's important for Christians to serve others in their work

50% of Millennials feel called to their work

EARLY CAREER

Climbing the ladder

75% of Millennials are always looking for ways to improve

69% of Millennials say it's important to find a job with opportunity to advance

33% of Millennials are willing to take major professional risks

26% of Millennials plan to continue their education in their line of work

Gen X is making its way through the middle of the work-life balance tightrope, and not without compromises. Meanwhile, Christian Boomers are transitioning out of full-time career mode feeling mostly satisfied with their well-being and relationships.

80% of Boomers use their unique talents outside of work in some capacity

59% of Boomers hold full-time roles

52% of Boomers earn enough to be financially secure, and then some

37% of Boomers prioritize giving charitably as an ultimate financial goal

Moving on

MID-CAREER

LATE CAREER

Finding balance

61% of Gen X are married

50% of Gen X are working parents with children at home

39% of Gen X are very satisfied with their true friendships

34% of Gen X are very satisfied with their quality of life

n=1,403 employed U.S. Christians.

2

WHEN FAITH & WORK
ARE INTEGRATED

"Work is the natural exercise and function of man—the creature
who is made in the image of his Creator." —*Dorothy Sayers*

The Bible begins with a model for work. In Genesis, we read of God forming the heavens and the earth and everything in them (an entrepreneur if there ever was one). We also meet Adam, placed "in the Garden of Eden to work it and take care of it" (2:15). These early scriptures introduce humans as lovingly created in God's image, tasked with shaping culture and intended for community, both with God and with one another.

In the passages to come, following the fall, the original design of work—a fruitful cycle of creation and rest—becomes something tedious and burdensome. But that's not the last thing the Bible has to say about work. Elsewhere, Christians are given instruction for redeeming work and extracting not only provision, but also purpose from daily labor. "May the favor of the Lord our God rest on us; establish the work of our hands for us," the Psalmist writes (90:17). New Testament writers speak of individual spiritual gifts (1 Peter 4:1–11), fruits of the Spirit (Galatians 5:22–23and disciples who don't hesitate to respond to a calling from Christ (Matthew 4:18–22). Several of Jesus' well-

known sermons and parables warn against hiding talents and inspire followers to be faithful servants and stewards in the Kingdom of God. Paul praises leading a quiet, hard-working life (1 Thessalonians 4:11), reminding us to do everything "in the name of the Lord Jesus, giving thanks to God the Father through him" (Colossians 3:17). And Peter challenges, "Each of you should use whatever gift you have received to serve others, as faithful stewards of God's grace in its various forms" (1 Peter 4:10).

What does it look like to respond to these scriptural teachings—using our individual callings in service of a broader Christian calling, embodying God's love through our occupations, our unique talents and our daily lives? Certainly, that's a moving target dependent on the timeline and context of each individual life.

One of this study's primary goals is to identify the Christians who demonstrate a high intentionality toward cultivating their vocation via their profession and experiencing an alignment of calling and career. Especially in a Western culture that is increasingly both post-Christian and career-oriented, we believe this faith-driven approach to one's work is to be commended by the Church. So we took a twofold approach to observe and measure to what extent Christians are actually integrating their faith and work. First, we conducted a series of qualitative interviews with workers who exhibit exemplary leadership and thinking in this area—some of which are highlighted in this report's "Conversations with Practitioners" and analyzed further on page 72. Then, building upon insights from these interviews and seeking to create an operational definition for some of the spiritual concepts mentioned above, we centered the quantitative analysis around some of the big questions that we all might ask ourselves in our careers.

Barna scored and grouped individuals based on their combined responses to these four statements:

> " I can clearly see how the work that I am doing is serving God or a higher purpose."

> " I find purpose and meaning in the work I do."

> " I am looking to make a difference in the world."

> " As a Christian, I believe it is important to help mold the culture of my workplace."

Christians who agree strongly with these attitudes are referred to by Barna as **Integrators** of faith and work. At the opposite end of the spectrum are **Compartmentalizers**, who express a low level of agreement with these mindsets. In the middle are **Onlookers**, with whom these ideas moderately resonate.

Christian Workers and Faith-Work Integration Types
Proportion among Christian workers

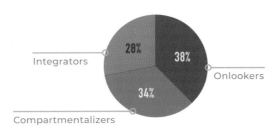

Integrators 28%

Onlookers 38%

Compartmentalizers 34%

n=1,459 employed U.S. Christians.

Measuring Faith-Work Integration Attitudes
% strongly agree

◆ Compartmentalizers   ◆ Onlookers   ◆ Integrators   ◆ All Christians

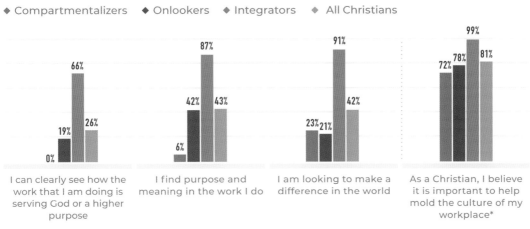

I can clearly see how the work that I am doing is serving God or a higher purpose — 0%, 19%, 66%, 26%

I find purpose and meaning in the work I do — 6%, 42%, 87%, 43%

I am looking to make a difference in the world — 23%, 21%, 91%, 42%

As a Christian, I believe it is important to help mold the culture of my workplace* — 72%, 78%, 99%, 81%

n=1,459 employed U.S. Christians
Total level of agreement: "completely" + "somewhat".

This report will contain more details about Onlookers and Compartmentalizers in the following chapter, but in hopes of putting forth a model for a deeply vocational approach to work, we'll start by examining faith-work Integrators, an exemplary minority (28%) among Barna's sample of Christian workers. Their professional ethos overwhelmingly stands out from the rest and is correlated with a willingness to invest skills and resources wisely, take considered risks, look for ways to improve and work for the good of others. In the process, Integrators gain perspective on the world outside their cubicles (or hospital wings, fields, classrooms, home offices, etc.) and connect with the God who made work good.

THE SPECTRUM OF FAITH-WORK INTEGRATION

Barna has defined three vocational personalities among Christian workers. Here's a look at some of their key attitudes about their calling and career.

◆ Compartmentalizers
◆ Onlookers
◆ Integrators

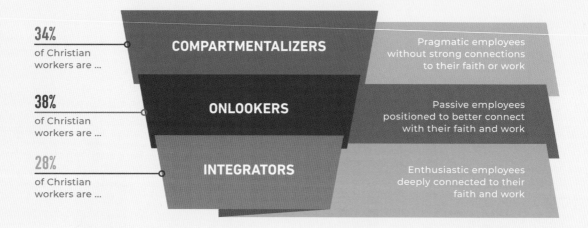

34%
of Christian workers are …

COMPARTMENTALIZERS

Pragmatic employees without strong connections to their faith or work

38%
of Christian workers are …

ONLOOKERS

Passive employees positioned to better connect with their faith and work

28%
of Christian workers are …

INTEGRATORS

Enthusiastic employees deeply connected to their faith and work

The Big Ideas Behind the Definitions
% strongly agree

"I can clearly see how the work I'm doing serves God or a higher purpose."

 0%   19%   66%

"I am looking to make a difference in the world."

 23%   21%   91%

"I find purpose and meaning in the work I do."

 6%   42%   87%

"As a Christian, it is important to mold the culture of my workplace."

 22%   20%   72%

In Several Key Dimensions, Integrators Stand Out

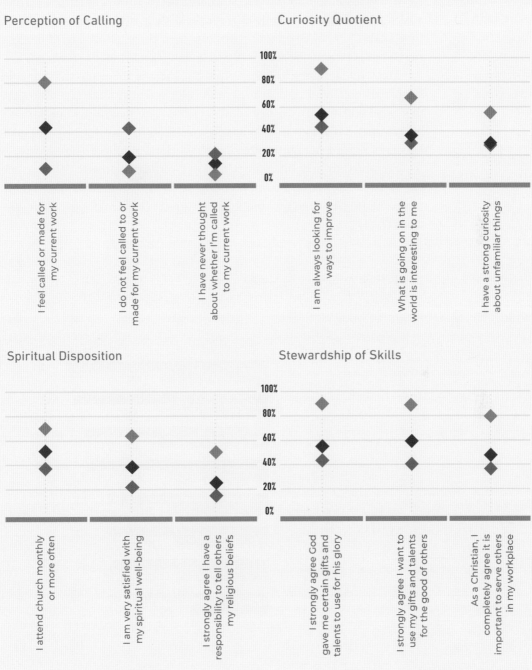

Perception of Calling

I feel called or made for my current work

I do not feel called to or made for my current work

I have never thought about whether I'm called to my current work

Curiosity Quotient

I am always looking for ways to improve

What is going on in the world is interesting to me

I have a strong curiosity about unfamiliar things

Spiritual Disposition

I attend church monthly or more often

I am very satisfied with my spiritual well-being

I strongly agree I have a responsibility to tell others my religious beliefs

Stewardship of Skills

I strongly agree God gave me certain gifts and talents to use for his glory

I strongly agree I want to use my gifts and talents for the good of others

As a Christian, I completely agree it is important to serve others in my workplace

n=1,459 employed U.S. Christians.

WORK IS WORKING FOR INTEGRATORS

Integrators see their work as purposeful and a good fit, and this pattern holds throughout their responses

By Barna's definition, faith-work Integrators see their work as purposeful and a good fit, and this pattern holds throughout their responses. A majority of Integrators (77%) feels called to or made for their current work, and 68 percent say they are very satisfied with how well their work matches their calling.

Most Integrators give themselves high scores for using their unique strengths and talents in their paid work (74% agree "strongly") and say that their work aligns well with their educational backgrounds (91% agree "strongly" + "somewhat"). This is undoubtedly a relief for this particularly educated bunch, as 59 percent of Integrators have some kind of college degree.

Presently, six in 10 Integrators (60%) are very satisfied with their current job, and, looking ahead, similar proportions feel very optimistic about their prospects (61%) or the way their current role is preparing them for future plans (70%).

Vocational Satisfaction Is High Among Integrators

◆ Integrators ◆ All Christian workers

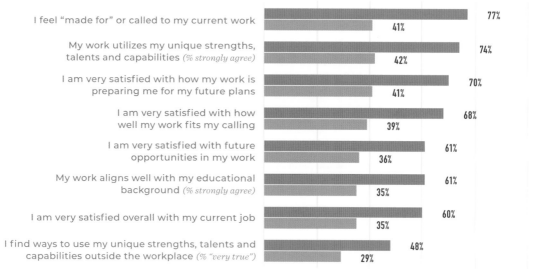

	Integrators	All Christian workers
I feel "made for" or called to my current work	77%	41%
My work utilizes my unique strengths, talents and capabilities (% strongly agree)	74%	42%
I am very satisfied with how my work is preparing me for my future plans	70%	41%
I am very satisfied with how well my work fits my calling	68%	39%
I am very satisfied with future opportunities in my work	61%	36%
My work aligns well with my educational background (% strongly agree)	61%	35%
I am very satisfied overall with my current job	60%	35%
I find ways to use my unique strengths, talents and capabilities outside the workplace (% "very true")	48%	29%

n=1,459 employed U.S. Christians.

If Integrators are thriving in their work, is it because other aspects of their lives take a backseat? The answer seems to be a resounding *no*. First of all, their vocational fulfillment is not limited to their profession; nearly half of Integrators (48%) say it's very true that they find ways to apply their strengths and skills even in non-work contexts—almost 20 percentage points more than all working Christians (29%). But beyond this measure, this study indicates that satisfying personal lives correspond to satisfying work lives and a sense of vocation.

Integrators' responses show a relationship between high expectations and high rewards. They tend to rate their well-being at the highest level—not only generally (59% with overall quality of life), but also socially (70% with family relationships, 63% with having true friends), mentally (66% with mental health, 56% with emotional health) and spiritually (64% with their spiritual well-being).

Satisfying personal lives correspond to satisfying work lives and a sense of vocation

Integrators Thrive Beyond the Workplace Too

How satisfied are you right now when it comes to each of the following in your life?

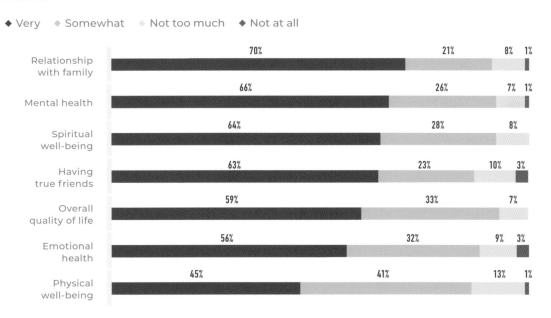

◆ Very   ◆ Somewhat   ◆ Not too much   ◆ Not at all

	Very	Somewhat	Not too much	Not at all
Relationship with family	70%	21%	8%	1%
Mental health	66%	26%	7%	1%
Spiritual well-being	64%	28%	8%	
Having true friends	63%	23%	10%	3%
Overall quality of life	59%	33%	7%	
Emotional health	56%	32%	9%	3%
Physical well-being	45%	41%	13%	1%

n=381 faith-work Integrators.

Integrators and All Christians Share a Vision—But Integrators Want to Lead

In a seminal study on evidence of a sense of calling among zookeepers, J. Stuart Bundersen and Jeffrey A. Thompson describe "calling" as a blend of destiny and duty, or of self-focused and society-focused ideals. They write, "Zookeepers therefore pursue their calling not because they enjoy cleaning cages, but, rather, because cleaning cages is part of their offering to society, an offering they feel obligated to make because of their particular gifts and society's needs."[34]

Barna was curious to learn what Christians expect when they imagine the work they are "made for"—what are the needs of self or society that they might address, as well as the workaday obligations of fulfilling those needs? Overall, the working Christians in this study, including the Integrators of faith and work, look forward to a job description that is enriching and exciting, though they seem well aware there will inevitably be some cages to clean.

First, there is a consensus among all Christians that when a person does the work they are made for, they will use their natural talents and have enough to live comfortably, plan for the future and help others financially. However, Integrators diverge somewhat from all Christians in anticipating chances to lead, such as being their own bosses (69% vs. 60%) or managing others (69% vs. 60%). They are also slightly more inclined to envision a career that includes travel (73% vs. 67%) or even a certain level of fame (21% vs. 16%). (Hopefully, this latter assumption is anchored by the humility and altruism that Integrators exhibit elsewhere.)

Amid their grander goals, Integrators are still open to the rigorous or even mundane aspects of a calling. Challenging tasks, long hours and a fast-paced environment are all presumed—though, as Americans know, it can be tempting to glamorize "the hustle" as part of the career journey or proof of a hard-won calling. Just as long as it never gets boring:

LET'S TALK ABOUT ... WHAT INTEGRATING FAITH & WORK LOOKS LIKE

❝ I challenge everybody to struggle with that integration of faith and work. You should be questioning, *How did I represent today? At the very least, how did I represent God? How did I represent the Church today? Secondarily, did the fruits of my labor contribute?*"

—*Dean Batali, film and TV producer*

❝ To listen to people, to be an ear, and to create community—I think that's the purpose. Hopefully, through the chair and through loving and understanding and listening to people, they would, to put it in Christian terms, 'see Christ through me.' And they would see that and want to experience it for their own lives."

—*David Martinez, barber shop owner*

Imagining the Ideal Role

If I were able to do the work I was "made for," I would probably ...

◆ Integrators   ◆ All Christian workers

Expectations for ...

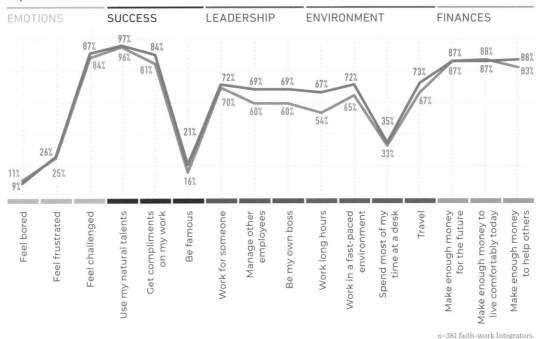

EMOTIONS · SUCCESS · LEADERSHIP · ENVIRONMENT · FINANCES

- Feel bored — 11% / 9%
- Feel frustrated — 26% / 25%
- Feel challenged — 87% / 84%
- Use my natural talents — 97% / 96%
- Get compliments on my work — 84% / 81%
- Be famous — 21% / 16%
- Work for someone — 72% / 70%
- Manage other employees — 69% / 60%
- Be my own boss — 69% / 60%
- Work long hours — 67% / 54%
- Work in a fast-paced environment — 72% / 65%
- Spend most of my time at a desk — 35% / 33%
- Travel — 73% / 67%
- Make enough money for the future — 87% / 87%
- Make enough money to live comfortably today — 88% / 87%
- Make enough money to help others — 88% / 83%

n=381 faith-work Integrators.

> ❝ It is my duty as a Christian artist raising the next generation of Christian artists to protect them from bad art, just as much as it is to protect them from bad theology. I want to make sure that I'm telling compelling stories as well as convicting stories, that I'm creating embraceable, recognizable characters who are going to make people think and they're going to make people feel. And if I'm lucky, they're going to shake people up a little bit."
>
> —*Sheryl J. Anderson, television writer*

Conversations with Practitioners

Integrators diverge
from all Christians
in anticipating
chances to lead

This is the thing that Integrators, like all Christian workers, are least likely to assume will be a factor in their ideal occupation.

DEMOGRAPHIC DETAILS: WHO ARE THE INTEGRATORS?

You might be wondering: Are faith-work Integrators just ... privileged? Maybe lucky? After all, this group seems to have found meaningful work and anticipate further influence in an unfair world. Not only is it rare to have a "dream job," but resources and opportunity are also unevenly distributed among Americans. For example, women are promoted much more slowly than men, particularly if they are women of color.[35] Tall workers earn more than short workers.[36] Even adequate employment eludes many U.S. workers. Half of U.S. workers earn an hourly wage of $18.74 or less.[37] The mean annual earnings are $50,620[38]—less than what a family of four needs to make ends meet in many states.[39]

Nevertheless, there are reasons to believe that Integrators are not a group of people who have had outsized advantages. For instance, the demographic spread by factors like gender or socioeconomic status does not vary significantly when looking at Integrators compared to Barna's total sample of working Christians. Integrators do skew toward being more educated—41 percent have an undergraduate or higher degree. But even with these academic achievements, there are no significant differences between the

LET'S TALK ABOUT ... WHAT INTEGRATING FAITH & WORK LOOKS LIKE

❝ I think that the way to be the best example of living out your faith in the marketplace is to do incredible quality work and create products and services that are like the top one percent. And then that gives you the right to talk, and people will listen to you. And then that leads to questions."
—*Woody Faulk, vice president of innovation & new ventures for Chick-fil-A*

❝ You can be called to be a plumber or a fisherman or a venture capitalist,

household income of Integrators and all Christian workers, one indicator that Integrators' positivity and passion about work and vocation can't simply be chalked up to higher earnings.

Generationally, Integrators include a greater-than-average proportion of Millennials (38%), on par with Gen X (39%) and ahead of Boomers (22%). By comparison, Millennials (26%) and Boomers (29%) have more equal representation among workers who don't qualify as Integrators of faith and work (compared to 42% Gen X). There could be an impulse for young respondents to overestimate their own aspirations and principles or over-identify with career success, thus qualifying more easily as Integrators in Barna's metric. But Millennials' strong presence as Integrators might also be another example of how younger adults naturally focus more attention on growing into a profession, while other priorities move to the foreground as individuals age. Additionally, the plurality of Integrators is Gen X, a sign that many of those in the thick of balancing career-building with child-rearing (59% of Gen X have kids under 18 at home) are doing so with sincere attention to the impact of their work and calling.

Ultimately, Barna's survey questions aren't focused on the effect of a person's status, influence or earnings, but on what a person looks for and finds both in themselves and in their jobs. Among this exceptional and inclusive segment of Integrators, it is impossible to untangle the relationship between experiencing a job as a good fit and having a hopeful attitude; they band together, one positive idea reinforcing the other.

> Integrators' positivity and passion about work and vocation can't simply be chalked up to higher earnings

as long as you live your values and faith through what you do—that's what matters. We need more Christians to approach their work this way and not decouple their faith from their vocation."

—*Phil Graves, senior director of corporate development for Patagonia*

66 [My work] is the Kingdom; it's new creation. I am new creation. God is pruning and refining me to inspire, but whatever is left, my identity in Christ, is the new creation. My job is to bring that out in my art."

—*Makoto Fujimura, artist, writer*

Conversations with Practitioners

5 HALLMARKS OF THE INTEGRATORS' APPROACH TO WORK

Though the results of this study can't speak to the actual work ethic, impact or daily performance of these employees, it does reveal some complementary relationships between faith-work Integrators' standards and their well-being, which all Christians can learn from. In the following pages, we've encapsulated some of the trends and attitudes that most characterize Integrators' presence and engagement in the workplace.

Integrators are more likely to regard faith as the foundation of their identity

1. Work Is Spiritual

If these Christians are so profoundly deliberate about their work, you might think that their profession, accomplishment or title is very central to their sense of self. However, the distinction between them and others seems to be that Integrators are more likely to regard faith as the foundation of their identity.

Given this, Integrators—two-thirds of whom (66%) are practicing Christians—consistently acknowledge God as having a role in the work they do and in their vocation generally. Nine in 10 Integrators (89%) agree strongly

Integrators' Work Keeps God in Mind
% strongly agree

◆ Integrators ◆ All Christian workers

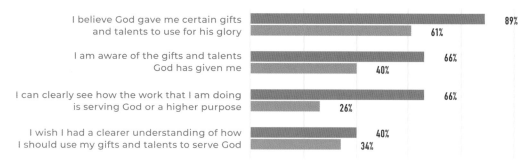

I believe God gave me certain gifts and talents to use for his glory	89% / 61%
I am aware of the gifts and talents God has given me	66% / 40%
I can clearly see how the work that I am doing is serving God or a higher purpose	66% / 26%
I wish I had a clearer understanding of how I should use my gifts and talents to serve God	40% / 34%

n=1,459 employed U.S. Christians.

that God has given them talents to use for his glory—28 percentage points more than all Christians (61%). Two-thirds of Integrators are acutely aware of these God-given gifts (66%) and can clearly see how their work is serving God or a higher purpose (66%). And even with this higher-than-average awareness, they are still seeking greater understanding of their calling (40%).

Integrators see connections not only between God and their work, but between God and others' work. For every job included in the survey—from entertainment executives to school janitors—they are more likely to see its potential as a calling or a chance to contribute to the common good. A majority (56%) says neither going into ministry nor representing your faith well at work is the better choice

for Christians, but they are less likely than all Christians (64%) to feel this way, and slightly more likely to lean toward pursuing faithful living in the marketplace (16% vs. 12%). It's possible that this group simply has more definitive ideas about what a line of work represents and is less drawn to a "neither" response.

2. Set the Bar High

When asked about the qualities that are important for finding or staying in a particular job, Integrators are more likely than others to see high value in all of the possible job characteristics Barna presented. At the top of their list of criteria is a job's ability to contribute to personal satisfaction (84%) or the greater good of society and the world (73%), followed by practical concerns like competitive pay and

Integrators' Priorities Start with the Heart

How important are each of the following when it comes to finding or staying in a particular job?

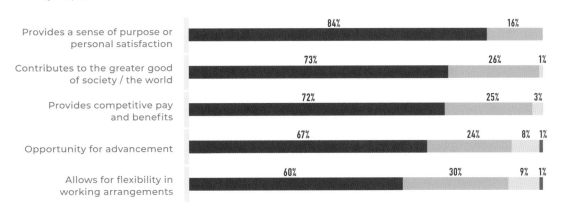

◆ Very important   ◆ Somewhat important   ◆ Not too important   ◆ Not at all important

	Very important	Somewhat important	Not too important	Not at all important
Provides a sense of purpose or personal satisfaction	84%	16%		
Contributes to the greater good / the world	73%	26%	1%	
Provides competitive pay and benefits	72%	25%	3%	
Opportunity for advancement	67%	24%	8%	1%
Allows for flexibility in working arrangements	60%	30%	9%	1%

n=381 faith-work Integrators.

benefits (72%), opportunity for advancement (67%) and flexibility in work arrangements (60%).

If Integrators require more of their jobs, they also require more of themselves—as workers and as people of faith. When shown a range of activities or offerings that Christians might be called to bring into the workplace, Integrators feel strongly that *all* of these endeavors are important, at consistently higher percentages than the average Christian worker. This is especially true of molding the culture of their workplace (72% vs. 35% of all working Christians) and sharing the gospel (44% vs. 24%)—a sign that these influencers' desire to make a difference is still accompanied by a boldness in their faith, even in a time when spiritual conversations are increasingly rare and 77 percent of Christians prefer to communicate about God through their lives, not their words.[40] Accordingly, Integrators hope to make friends with non-Christian colleagues (78%) and bring grace and peace to others (75%). These exemplars feel compelled to be an instrument of "common grace for the common good."[41]

> These influencers' desire to make a difference is still accompanied by a boldness in their faith, even in a time when spiritual conversations are increasingly rare

What Are Christian Responsibilities in the Workplace?
% "completely" important

◆ Integrators   ◆ All Christian workers

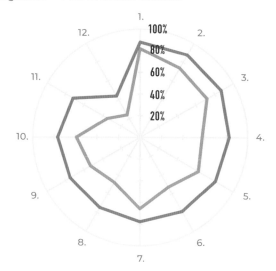

1. Act ethically
2. Always speak the truth
3. Demonstrate morality
4. Do excellent work to glorify God
5. Practice humility
6. Serve others
7. Make friends with non-Christians
8. Help bring grace and peace to others
9. Speak out against unfairness or injustice
10. Withstand temptation
11. Help mold the culture of my workplace
12. Share the gospel

n=1,459 employed U.S. Christians.

Encouragingly, this same group holds standards of professional integrity that the Church would be well represented by. Integrators are rooted in a conviction that Christians should act ethically (88%), speak the truth (88%) demonstrate morality (87%) and confront injustice (75%) in the workplace. Eighty-three percent believe that people of faith have a responsibility to do excellent work in an effort to bring glory to God. On a more personal, spiritual level, they say working Christians should be guided by an attitude of humility (81%) and service (79%).

Sadly, faith-work Integrators' professional principles are even more exceptional in contrast to some from the total sample in Barna's survey. For example, a little over half of working Christians (53%) place a high importance on speaking out against unfairness and injustice, more than 20 percentage points behind Integrators. Given that this survey was issued in early 2018, after the rise of the #MeToo movement and amid scandals highlighting the prevalence of misogyny and assault in multiple industries, one might expect the idea of workplace injustice to feel more urgent to respondents—particularly Christians commanded to "do justice and love kindness" (Micah 6:8). As broader culture and the Church at large determine how to hold leaders accountable and build companies and ministries that are fair, respectful and safe, Integrators might need to lead their fellow Christians and colleagues in being proactive.

3. You've Never Truly "Made It"

Integrators approach their career as a meandering path with multiple outcomes, rather than a straight course with one end goal. Thus, they stand out in their willingness to embrace a variety of possibilities and lifelong learning.

First of all, Integrators don't just have more education than the average Christian worker, they also *want* more education.

Integrators Contemplate Multiple Opportunities

When you think about the things you might do in your life (whether career, individual projects or anything else), how would you describe yourself?

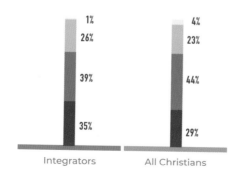

1%
26%
39%
35%
Integrators

4%
23%
44%
29%
All Christians

◆ I don't really know what I want to do with my life
◆ I am primarily focused on one or two main roles or types of work
◆ I can think of a few things I'd like to pursue
◆ I can think of many things I'd like to do; it's difficult to choose one

n=1,459 employed U.S. Christians.

Even with their academic achievements, Integrators remain very open to continuing their education in their current line of work (58% vs. 38% select "definitely" + "probably"), or perhaps even to change their line of work (26% vs. 20% select "definitely").

Though they are about as likely as others to say they are primarily focused on one or two main roles or types of work (26% vs. 23% of all Christians), Integrators find it especially difficult to choose among the many things they'd like to do (35%). But they are actively seeking clarity from God in this regard; 40 percent agree strongly that they wish they had a greater understanding about how they should be serving him with their skills. Appropriately, when asked to imagine their professional future, Integrators offer a semi-focused picture of possibilities.

As you can see, even though they have more aspirations or expectations for their role in the marketplace, Integrators still seem a bit restless. Perhaps an intense awareness of their own gifts opens up multiple possibilities, or maybe, because of their desire to produce change and impact, Integrators are often self-monitoring for continued optimization of their talents. One way or another, most Integrators never feel that they are done growing. Ninety-one percent—compared to 61 percent of all Christians—agree strongly that they are always looking for ways to improve. And many other studies suggest a vision for meaningful work *should* be a malleable one. As career coach Stephanie Shackelford writes, "The adaptability to think ahead and prepare for the future, while remaining open to new ideas and plans, is a key part of developing a career calling."[42]

4. Embrace Curiosity & Risk

A strong desire for self-improvement is just one part of a "curiosity quotient" that Barna observed in this study. Curiosity has a number of positive effects on a person's ability to improve workplaces and society. It has been linked to resilience in relationships,[43] less political polarization[44] and handling conflict well,[45] among other benefits. In this study, Integrators are more likely than other Christian workers to exhibit characteristics of curiosity. More than two-thirds (68%) strongly agree that what is going on in the world is interesting to them, compared to 45 percent of all Christians who feel this way. Fifty-six percent of Integrators confidently describe themselves as curious about unfamiliar things, also well exceeding all Christians (38%).

This enthusiasm is reflected in Integrators' openness to taking chances professionally. As Barna explores in detail on page 69, entrepreneurship doesn't necessarily characterize the majority of Integrators—however, this is by no means a particularly risk-averse segment. Integrators show that they are comfortable putting themselves out there not only in their occupations, but toward other life goals and projects as well. Integrators are much more likely than the average Christian to say they are willing to take major risks (37% vs. 22%) and less likely to express hesitation about taking such leaps of faith (17% vs. 26%).

Integrators Keep an Open Mind

◆ Agree strongly   ◆ Agree somewhat   ◆ Disagree somewhat   ◆ Disagree strongly

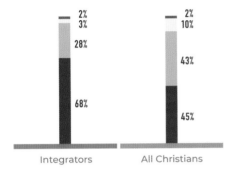

*"What is going on in the world
is interesting to me"*

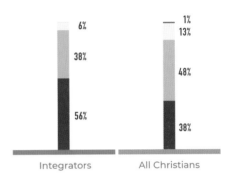

*"I have a strong curiosity about
unfamiliar things"*

n=1,459 employed U.S. Christians.

Integrators Are Ready to Put Themselves out There

*When you think about all of the things you want do in your life (whether career,
individual projects or anything else), would you say you are …?*

◆ Willing to take major risks to pursue
these things
◆ Willing to take minor risks to pursue
these things

◆ Hesitant to take risks to pursue these things
◆ Not interested in taking risks to pursue
these things

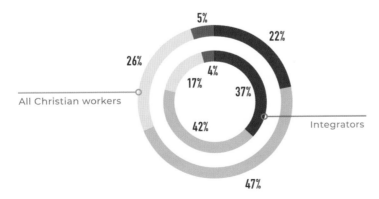

n=1,459 employed U.S. Christians.

5. Don't Bury Your Talents

In Bryan Dik and Ryan Duffy's writings about the psychology of calling, their preferred definition of the term is distinctly selfless: "a transcendent summons, experienced as originating beyond the self, to approach a particular life role in a manner oriented toward demonstrating or deriving a sense of purpose or meaningfulness and that holds other-oriented values and goals as primary sources of motivation."[46] This altruistic interpretation pairs well with the profile of Integrators, who respect their unique calling and capability as something that should be cultivated to enrich the lives of others, not just their own.

In addition to their distinctive characteristic of looking to make a difference in the world, most Integrators (88% vs. 61% of all Christian workers) agree strongly that they want to use their gifts for the good of others, perhaps one manifestation of their strong belief that these talents are given by God to use for his glory (89% vs. 61% of all Christian workers). This open-handedness and selflessness seem to be defining traits of faith-work Integrators.

The Integrators' generous stewardship extends to their finances as well. Though they align with all Christian workers (59% and 61%, respectively) in considering providing for their families as the ultimate financial goal, many Integrators also aim to serve God with their money (45%). In addition, they are less likely to prioritize earning money in order to support the lifestyle that they want (24% vs. 30%).

Like Christians overall (57%), they regard stewardship as a combination of using the earth's resources wisely, giving an offering to church and using their God-given talents (63%). Integrators are more likely, though, to find ways to express their generosity through service and volunteering (34% vs. 26% of all Christians).

> Open-handedness and selflessness seem to be defining traits of faith-work Integrators

Integrators See Their Gifts as Gifts to God and Others

◆ Agree strongly   ◆ Agree somewhat   ◆ Disagree somewhat

I believe God gave me certain gifts and talents to use for his glory — 89% 10% 1%

I want to use my gifts and talents for the good of others — 88% 11%

n=381 faith-work Integrators.

Ultimate Financial Goals of All Christians and Integrators

Select up to three

◆ Integrators ◆ All Christian workers

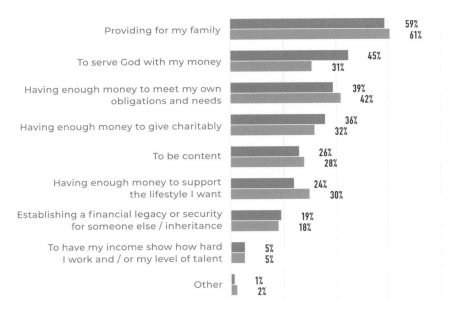

Providing for my family — 59% / 61%

To serve God with my money — 45% / 31%

Having enough money to meet my own obligations and needs — 39% / 42%

Having enough money to give charitably — 36% / 32%

To be content — 26% / 28%

Having enough money to support the lifestyle I want — 24% / 30%

Establishing a financial legacy or security for someone else / inheritance — 19% / 18%

To have my income show how hard I work and / or my level of talent — 5% / 5%

Other — 1% / 2%

n=1,459 employed U.S. Christians.

What Does Stewardship Mean to All Christians and Integrators?

◆ Integrators ◆ All Christian workers

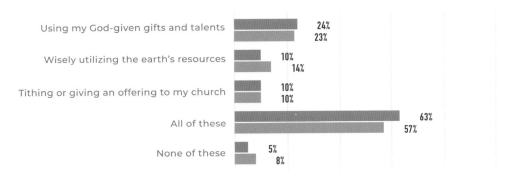

Using my God-given gifts and talents — 24% / 23%

Wisely utilizing the earth's resources — 10% / 14%

Tithing or giving an offering to my church — 10% / 10%

All of these — 63% / 57%

None of these — 5% / 8%

n=1,459 employed U.S. Christians.

THE KINGDOM COMING NEAR

Why integration of faith and work is one answer to the Church's waning influence

BY DR. BEN RIES

As I read about the ways in which people integrate their faith with their work, I am reminded of a story in Luke's gospel of Jesus sending out 70 disciples to heal the sick and announce the Kingdom of God coming near. Jesus sends them in pairs to "every town and place that he himself intended to go" (10:1). The disciples are instructed to take very little for the journey—no purse, no bag, and no sandals (v. 3–4). They are invited to find people of peace and stay in their homes, relying on their hospitality for food, shelter and company (v. 8). It is a radical vision of evangelism where God's Kingdom comes near, not on the terms and turf of the disciples, but of the people to whom they are sent.

This is something with which most of us in the American Church are unfamiliar. Ministry, programs and evangelism tend to happen on the local church's terms and turf. People are invited to our buildings on Sunday morning to worship in song, hear the good news through a lesson and respond with a proclamation of faith. We invite them to marriage seminars, classes on effective parenting or a game night that our church is hosting, all while looking for creative ways to share the news that God loves them. Nearly all of these efforts require others to take the journey from their homes and rely on the hospitality of church members and leaders. And who could blame us? We have delicious cookies and micro-roasted coffee to offer. Even our efforts of evangelism that take place in the workplace, neighborhood pubs, community centers and streets where we live tend to treat the local church as the end goal. We hope that these efforts outside the walls of the church will eventually bring people back to our buildings, worship and ministries so that they can participate, tithe and help our efforts to do the same for others.

Don't be mistaken; these are all good things. The Church has effectively proclaimed God's love for creation and God's longing for humanity to receive and respond to the good news for centuries. The love, acceptance and community that many have experienced through the efforts of the Church is no small thing. And yet the Church in North America is coming to terms with a pretty harsh reality: It no longer has the voice, power and influence it once had. Ministries and programs that once were so successful no longer get the same results. Congregations struggle to meet their budgets, pay their pastors and keep their doors open. Add to this the number of people who identify as "nones"—those individuals who choose no religious affiliation—and the crisis facing the Church feels daunting.

The temptation is to do what we've always done, just better. We rebrand the church website, find a new worship leader, throw some trendier clothes on the lead pastor and try to make existing programs flashier and more impressive. The problem we soon discover is that while we are able to do ministry and programs better—or at least cooler—than ever, we are experiencing diminishing returns. Our best efforts to make the local church more accessible, attractive and engaging often leave us with a strong sense that we are accomplishing something but very little evidence that our testimony is any more effective than it was before.

The good news is that there are those among us from whom we can learn a different way. There are men and women who sit in our pews who walk into board meetings, classrooms, warehouses, offices and interactions with clients with a deep sense that God is there and that God is up to something in this world. They are teachers, lawyers, executives, non-profit leaders, social workers and health-care professionals who have developed a sense that their work is not simply something to endure, but the very place they experience God's presence and transforming power. Like the 70 sent in Luke 10, they go to their places of work expecting to find people of peace from whom they can learn and on whom they can depend. They see their work not as a means to an end—that is, a place to find people to bring to church; they see their work as the location where healing begins and God's Kingdom comes near.

DR. BEN RIES is the associate dean for vocational formation and director of the Center for Vocational Formation at Abilene Christian University. With over 18 years of ministry experience in the Pacific Northwest, Dr. Ries' work focuses on helping working professionals experience their work as meaningful and connected to the life and mission of God. He and his wife, Jen, live in Dallas with their three children.

As the Church wrestles with its diminishing voice and influence in politics, education and culture, we need these exemplars to show us a new way and give us new imagination. We need these Integrators of faith and work who approach their jobs with humility to teach

———

"[Integrators] have developed a sense that their work is not simply something to endure, but the very place they experience God's presence and transforming power."

———

the Church how to confess once more that we don't have all the answers and that there are those outside our walls from whom we have something to learn. We need these Integrators to teach the Church how to take risks and once

again trust that our life is not dependent on our ability to produce, manage or create ministries; our life is dependent on a risen Lord who sends us out ahead of him to every town and place he himself intends to go. We need these Integrators to help us release the tight grip we hold on our facilities, programs and ministries and live a more open-handed life as we embrace our identity as the sent people of God who carry very little for the journey, but still have all that we need.

It will not be easy or simple. We have much invested in how we have done church, and learning to release a few of our proverbial purses, bags and sandals for the journey ahead will not be easy and will require prayerful discernment. Yet if we can muster up the courage to learn from those who have gone before us, we might just discover that the intersection of our calling and career is the very place we join the disciples sent by Jesus long ago and proclaim, "The Kingdom of God has come near!"

STARTING SOMETHING

A Profile of Entrepreneurial Integrators

Though they certainly include industrious, innovative workers and leaders, those who scored highly for integrating calling and career aren't exceptionally entrepreneurial as a whole. Granted, they are more ambitious than their peers, but they're not defined as a group by this motivation. Just under half of faith-work Integrators (45%) strongly agree that they'd like to start their own business (compared to 30% of all Christians), and more than a quarter (28%) describes themselves as entrepreneurial (compared to 17% of all Christians).

In an effort to understand the vocational expressions of Christians who have (or at least desire) the opportunity to shape companies or even industries from the top down, Barna took a microscope to the Integrators who *do* tend to be more entrepreneurial—a small group of people who are willing to take risks and would like to start their own businesses, which makes up just 6 percent of the total sample.

For starters, entrepreneurial Integrators experience unusually strong curiosity about the world (87% "very") and willingness to

"I have already, or would like to, start my own business someday"

◆ Agree strongly ◆ Agree somewhat ◆ Disagree somewhat ◆ Disagree strongly

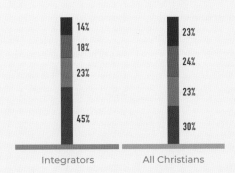

Integrators: 14%, 18%, 23%, 45%

All Christians: 23%, 24%, 23%, 30%

n=1,459 employed U.S. Christians.

Do you consider yourself **entrepreneurial**?

◆ Definitely   ◆ Somewhat   ◆ A little   ◆ Not really / not at all

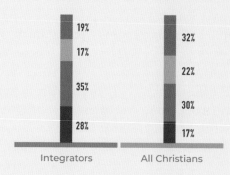

Integrators	All Christians
19%	32%
17%	22%
35%	30%
28%	17%

n=1,459 employed U.S. Christians.

make a difference within it (97% "strongly" agree)—important qualities for those envisioning new companies, services or products. In terms of employment, there are some industries that seem to be a better fit for this type of worker, like building trades and construction (17%, compared to 7% of all Integrators) or marketing and sales (13%, compared to 6% of all Integrators).

There is a notable gender gap among entrepreneurial Integrators; while all Integrators are split 56 percent male / 44 percent female, two-thirds of this more enterprising segment (65%) are men. This is to be expected, given some of the differences between the career priorities and experiences of men and women (explored more on page 34).

Entrepreneurial Integrators are slightly more motivated by the practical benefits of a job. They want to find—or create—a role that provides competitive pay (84% vs. 72%) and

would allow them to advance (76% vs. 63%). Though their overall financial goals don't vary significantly from all Integrators, their financial position does. Given both the risk and reward of starting a business, entrepreneurial Integrators are more likely to occupy either end of the self-sufficiency scale, whether requiring financial assistance (15% vs. 9%) or earning more than they need (24% vs. 12%)—a notable level of unpredictability among a group who typically still have children at home (61%).

Though one might assume that the demands of entrepreneurship would tax one's family and friendships, these entrepreneurs are perhaps aided by their Integrator values when it comes to maintaining relational well-being, even while building a business or career. Their level of satisfaction with their friends (70% "very") and family ties (74% "very") holds steady alongside all Integrators.

Interestingly, on one point, Integrators with an entrepreneurial bent are significantly more likely to perceive a boundary between the ministry and the marketplace. About three in 10 (29% vs. 16% of all Integrators) feel it's "definitely" better for a Christian to be a pastor or missionary instead of representing faith well in their work. This distinguishes them from all Integrators, more than half of whom (56% vs. 45% of entrepreneurial Integrators) say neither path is somehow better than the other. Considering the likelihood that entrepreneurs will seek out or experience influence in the marketplace, these Integrators might need help in recalling the spiritual value of their own endeavors, too. Thankfully, church leaders should have a chance to address this; a large majority of entrepreneurial Integrators who regularly attend church (79%) feels professional support from their church community, where they say they frequently learn about how to live out their faith on the job (82%).

CONVERSATIONS WITH PRACTITIONERS: IN SUMMARY

Candid lessons from Christian leaders and entrepreneurs in a range of industries

BY DR. STEPHANIE SHACKELFORD

In the early stages of this study, Barna conducted qualitative interviews with more than 30 individuals who connect their faith and their work. You've seen many of their quotes scattered throughout this report, in our "Conversations with Practitioners" feature. Some are consultants, work in the entertainment industry, have founded schools or own their own businesses. Their insights proved invaluable as the researchers moved into the quantitative phase of research, and now, as we reflect on the entire study, we can see that these leaders also embody many of the traits of the faith-work Integrator segment that emerged in the data. Interestingly, none of these interviewees seems to view themselves as exemplary; instead, they describe their callings as just one role God uses to bring his Kingdom to earth day by day.

As we conducted these interviews, four primary themes emerged, which present an emphasis on God's work above one's own and offer a glimpse of the "best practices" of those thinking deeply about vocation and effectively influencing a variety of industries:

Identity Is Found in Christ, Not Work

In addition to my work as a researcher, I am also a career coach, and my clients, regardless of their age, have been asking the same question since kindergarten: "What do I want to do?" During the qualitative interviews for this study, however, we heard a different question: "Who am I?" Primary answers given are identity words like *daughter, disciple* and *redeemed.* Though most recognize the value in self-awareness, they acknowledge that God knows us more intimately than we can even understand ourselves. This appears in the data as well, with faith-work Integrators applying their strengths and talents at work yet being unlikely to derive their identity from their career. The interviewees confirm this trend by surrendering control of their identities and thereby expanding God's call for their vocation to include all of their various roles in life—spouse, parent, friend and professional. Representative of the entire Integrator group, their vocational fulfillment spills over to non-work settings, with their identities rooted in their faith.

Calling Is Discerned in Community

From this foundational perspective, the leaders Barna interviewed naturally extend their callings beyond themselves. The majority is also entrepreneurial, called "to work on specific problems ... to restore specific areas of brokenness in the world." Like the entrepreneurial subset of faith-work Integrators, they exhibit curiosity toward the world, creative problem-solving and a desire for their work to contribute to others.

In previous research that I conducted on vocation, I found that a calling emerges from your struggles, giving purpose to your work as you seek to help others.[47] However, serving your neighbors requires engagement in community, just as recognizing needs necessitates entering into others'—and one's own—brokenness. Not surprisingly, every subject I spoke with for this report emphasized in-depth community to discern God's call and illuminate their vocations. In other words, they hear from God through others. Relationships formed inside or outside the church have been more transformative of their work than the Church's teachings on vocation or programmatic offerings. When rooted in intimate community, individuals are confronted with various perspectives and challenged to discern God's calling on their lives.

Our Work Is Part of a Broader Gospel Narrative

In my other vocational research, I saw that individuals who identify with having a career calling see the future as a question mark,

DR. STEPHANIE SHACKELFORD received her Ed.D. in Organizational Leadership from Northeastern University. She also graduated with a M.Ed. in Organizational Leadership and a B.S. in Human and Organizational Development from Vanderbilt University. In 2012, she founded two companies focused on coaching students and professionals in navigating their career paths. In addition to her companies, she is an adjunct instructor for Vanderbilt University's Doctor of Education program, and she also conducts research and consults with organizations primarily around the topics of human capital and vocational development. Shackelford served as an advisor to Barna in the research phase of this report.

yet still secure.[48] Likewise, the practitioners I interviewed suggest a confidence that God will shape plans to his will, to accomplish his purposes. These workers position their personal journeys as a part of the larger gospel story, seeking out God's redemptive narrative. Accordingly, they approach their vocations with adaptability. Most doubt that they will be in their particular profession forever because they view their callings as seasonal. Though their meandering career paths could be construed as restlessness, they are grounded in God's larger story, tracing a cohesive thread through each career turn.

On one key point, the personal, qualitative interviews offer a less rosy picture than the quantitative study: As reported in chapter three, a majority of churched Christian workers strongly agrees that their church helps them live out their faith at work, but the personal conversations I had with vocational leaders suggest that the Church still struggles with engaging people's occupations in meaningful ways. Though a third of pastors believes faith communities are essential in helping Christians discern their vocation, there was an impression in these interviews that the Church subtly elevates ministry-related jobs above other occupations, or that pastors apply the gospel only to home life and the Church, leaving individuals to wonder how their vocation fits into this narrative. One leader told me, "It's one of the things that pastors are least equipped to do and one of the questions that Millennials are most likely to ask." Certainly, these exemplars receive spiritual nourishment from their church communities and view their professional calling as integral to their overall spiritual health—but their responses suggest they have not received specific vocational discipleship.

Have Faith to Obey

Several practitioners refer to their callings as humbling experiences, representative of only one small part of the Church Body. In God's redemptive story, the focus is on God's work, not ours. Though many are entrepreneurs, they emphasize following God's will over leading a mission he set out for them. Even so, like the Integrator group explored in the data, they are proactive in taking risks to be obedient to their current call. They do not shy away from life's messiness, recognizing that through experimenting and failing, God is still at work. This reflects themes in my previous research on the topic: It is not enough to discern the call; you have to act.[49] As one leader shared, "There is no perfect moment to step into the call.'"

The qualitative interviewees echo that one's calling must be broader than one's work in order to truly answer, "Who am I in Christ?" As one told me, "Work is one of the best ways that the Lord uses to sanctify us." In this way, vocation should ultimately point to God's work and his redemption story. We are called to faith; he fulfills his purposes. ▰

DEVELOPING LASTING CHANGE

A Q&A with Shamichael Hallman

Q What does "calling" mean to you?

A Frederick Buechner is noted as saying, "the place God calls you to is the place where your deep gladness and the world's deep hunger meets." We move toward our calling when we recognize that Christ is the center of our gladness and the world's hunger. Additionally, scripture instructs us that we should use whatever gifts we have received to serve others.

I believe that all Christians should be mindful of the call God has placed on their lives. As children of God, we have all been blessed with a variety of skills, talents and gifts that we should use to impact our world and glorify God. And I think people who are in positions of authority or influence over others should stress the importance of identifying the call of God at every stage of life.

———

"People who are in positions of authority or influence over others should stress the importance of identifying the call of God at every stage of life."

———

Q Your work is focused on encouraging individuals to bring a Christian perspective to bear on global issues and questions through coding and creating technology. Is this complex in a post-Christian culture? Why is it crucial for those in the Church to embrace such opportunities for influence, especially in tech?

A We found that most of the people who attend our hackathons are eager to affect change in their communities and beyond. While individuals vary in educational and socioeconomic backgrounds, a desire to tackle global issues through a Christian lens is a common bond. Code for the Kingdom has mobilized more than 5,000 people to create technology that eradicates poverty, combats homelessness and supports victims of human trafficking. These Kingdom initiatives confront injustices, foster spiritual formation and spread the gospel throughout the world. It hasn't been difficult to get attendees to buy in because we are intentional about recognizing the unique gifts of each potential attendee, inviting them to a community of like-minded people and providing opportunities to use their gifts, skills and passions to create life-transforming technologies.

We've discovered that the Church has often been reluctant in joining us in these efforts, while many faith-driven non-profits and organizations have been willing to do so. It's crucial that the Church embrace opportunities like these because we can and should be leaders in this realm. We believe there are many people sitting in the pews each Sunday waiting be to engaged in this way. We have often wondered how much greater our impact could be if the Church fully embraced the work. It's my prayer that they will get involved as we move ahead.

SHAMICHAEL HALLMAN
Global leadership for Code for the Kingdom

Hallman is passionate about all things faith and technology. In 2014, he became a coorganizer for a faith-based hackathon called Code for the Kingdom. As a part of this movement, he helped organize hackathons all over the world. This work enabled him to travel to Nairobi, Kenya, in 2015 to work with a group of Christian technologists to help combat corruption in 2015. He is the author of *Hacked: How a Christian Hackathon Is Shifting Traditional Engagement Models and Creating an Ecosystem for Life-Transforming Technology.*

Q What shifts do you see in the ways people imagine or approach their career? How can Christians continue to emphasize spiritual values of personhood in the increasingly digital context we occupy as professionals and consumers?

A There are a number of shifts that are affecting the ways in which people imagine and approach possible career paths. One of those shifts is a growing desire to engage in work that is meaningful and significant. Meaningful work goes beyond being a cog in the machine or just a number; it involves having opportunities to create lasting change. Additionally, workers now place an equal premium on time and pay. Having the flexibility to work from different places outside of the office helps to contribute to an ever-increasing desire for work-life balance.

I think because Christians are more willing than ever to view their jobs as a mission field, we can emphasize personhood by being mindful of how we view and treat coworkers and customers and how we carry out the daily duties of work in various spaces. ◢

3

WORK & WORSHIP

"A church will be effective to the extent that it enables laypeople to live out their faith on the street." —*Doug Sherman and William Hendricks*

The term and concept of *vocation* has its origins in the Christian Church. Though the connotations and the world in which it is applied have changed significantly in the centuries since, local churches continue to bear the sacred responsibility of preparing Christians for their own vocational commitments and challenging them to see the work of their hands as holy and unique.

Thankfully, this report intimates that churches are taking this charge seriously and remain powerful partners in living out one's calling. As mentioned earlier, those with practicing faith have a deeper vocational

awareness and satisfaction. Overall, regular church attenders seem to both receive from and give to their churches often in relation to their God-given gifts.

The majority of churched Christians in this sample—meaning those who attend worship services monthly—strongly agrees that their churches help them understand how to live out their faith in the workplace (53% "strongly" agree). Nearly all of these Christians (80%) are at least interested in using their work-related gifts at their churches, including 39 percent who already do so. Regular attendees in turn feel their churches

Regular church attenders seem to both receive from and give to their churches often in relation to their God-given gifts

are supportive of them in their career (45% "definitely"), often by providing specific training on vocation (63%).

Practicing Christians—distinguished from general monthly attendees by a strong affirmation that faith is very important to them—tend to be even more vocationally nourished by their church. And, as mentioned previously, practicing Christians are well-represented among faith-work Integrators (66%); Integrators are actually almost twice as likely as other, non-Integrator Christians to have a church that they attend weekly (62% vs. 32%). This consistency translates into other spiritual investments as well.

Do Christians Feel Vocationally Supported by Churches?

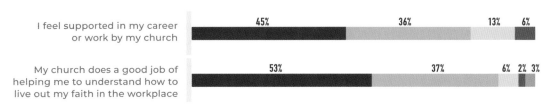

◆ Definitely   ◆ Somewhat   ◆ Not too much   ◆ Not at all   ◆ Not sure

	Definitely	Somewhat	Not too much	Not at all	Not sure
I feel supported in my career or work by my church	45%	36%	13%	6%	
My church does a good job of helping me to understand how to live out my faith in the workplace	53%	37%	6%	2%	3%

n≈734 employed U.S. Christians who attend church monthly.

Interest in Using Work-Related Gifts at Church

◆ Yes, currently doing so   ◆ Yes, I would like to   ◆ No

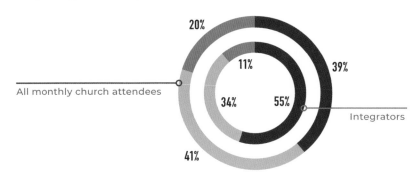

All monthly church attendees: 20% / 41% / 39%

Integrators: 11% / 34% / 55%

n≈734 employed U.S. Christians who attend church monthly.

Weekly Religious Activities of All Christians and Integrators

◆ Integrators ◆ All Christian workers

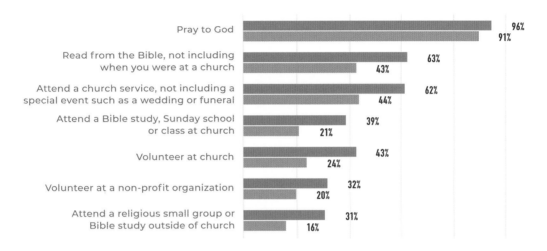

n=1,459 employed U.S. Christians.

Integrators' vision for living and working intentionally correlates with their deep faith and spiritual practices, as they outpace other Christian workers in weekly involvement in a variety of activities, from private prayer and Bible reading to community volunteering.

Some church-attending workers still point to barriers that keep them from getting more involved with their churches, the primary ones being professional (34%) or personal obligations (33%). Almost one-quarter (23%) says just being too tired holds them back from investing more in their faith community.

Interestingly, four in 10 among the highly motivated Integrators group (41%) say work gets in the way of church involvement, despite

the vocational backing they apparently receive from their churches and the 55 percent of Integrators who indicate they are in fact using their professional skillset to serve the Church. Highly engaged workers may be at a higher risk for burnout[50]—or, perhaps, for not meeting their own exceptional standards in every sphere of life. Integrators wanting to bring their best to their local congregations will need to be mindful of not over-exerting themselves in either their work or their church responsibilities. Additionally, ministries hoping to sustain faith-work Integrator engagement might want to focus on encouraging healthy work-life balance and long-term approaches to both vocational and spiritual development.

What Significantly Hinders Church Involvement?

◆ Integrators   ◆ All monthly church attendees

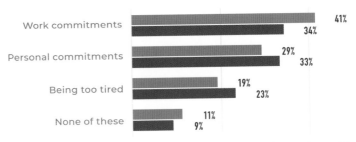

Work commitments — 41%
34%

Personal commitments — 29%
33%

Being too tired — 19%
23%

None of these — 11%
9%

n=734 employed U.S. Christians who attend church monthly.

Younger Workers Feel Support but Need Direction

A strong majority of each church-attending generation aims to serve their churches through their professional skillset (82% of Millennials, 80% of Gen X, 80% of Boomers). As Boomers lean into retirement, they aren't as confident in (or perhaps not as dependent on) their church for professional support (37% agree strongly), but a sense that church is a vocational asset trends upward among younger attendees (50% of Millennials, 46% of Gen X). Additionally, of working Christians who are in church at least monthly, Millennials more often report receiving sermons about work from their church (51% vs. 43% of Gen X and 31%

LET'S TALK ABOUT ... THE RELATIONAL ASPECTS OF VOCATION

❝ I think the Church's role is to foster intimate relationships. Obviously, we need an opportunity to worship. We need a place to hear good teachings and to have the Word illuminated to us. But I think one of the most important aspects is fostering that intimate community with people who can help you with that course correction."

—Heather Grizzle, founding partner of Causeway Strategies

❝ A lot of people, they have 5-year plans, but they don't have 50-year

of Boomers heard one in the last month)—a puzzling difference, presuming these groups are gathered in the same types of services. Some of this could depend on the makeup of a church body: If a congregation is generationally homogenous, are attendees more likely to receive spiritual instruction generally tailored to their age and time of life? Or is this a result of Millennials looking for (and, it seems, finding) what they most need in their present professional moment? Whatever Millennials actually hear, they aren't necessarily walking away from church feeling equipped with greater vocational understanding. Less than half say their church gives them a vision for living out their faith at work (46% vs. 57% of Gen X and 53% of Boomers agree "strongly").

Other responses from Christian Millennials imply they have some vocational lessons left to learn: When asked to point to values they should exhibit in the workplace, traits like speaking the truth, demonstrating morality, acting ethically or withstanding temptation diminish in importance among Millennials, particularly compared to Boomers. Even if younger Christian workers don't place the same level of importance on these spiritual opportunities in work, Millennials are still the most likely generation to say it's completely important for Christians to mold culture (40%, compared to 35% of Gen X and 33% of Boomers) or serve others (58%, compared to 51% of Gen X and 51% of Boomers) at their jobs.

Church leaders and mentors speaking into the professional development of younger adults should anticipate an audience eager for influence, but might want to be very specific about what it means to be a redemptive, Christ-like

> Responses from Christian Millennials imply they have some vocational lessons left to learn

plans. They don't have 500-year plans, which means you have to rely on the next generation to pass that on to multiple generations. We don't think that way, especially in America. Maybe we should."

—*Makoto Fujimura, artist, writer*

❝ Part of what I do is my business: We design buildings with excellence. Part of what I do is help the people who God has placed in my life to be the best version of themselves."

—*Darien M. Sykes, structural engineer, president of Sykes Consulting*

Conversations with Practitioners

Vocational Values, by Generation

As a Christian in my workplace, I believe it is completely important to ...

◆ Millennials   ◆ Gen X   ◆ Boomers

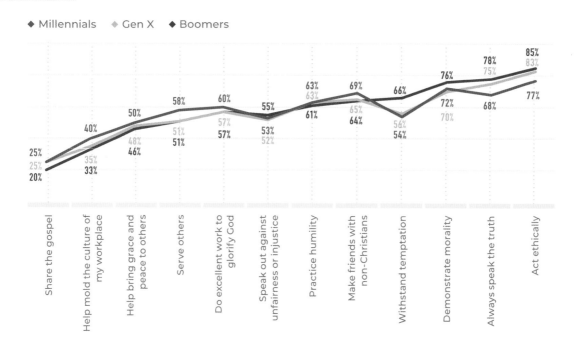

n≈1,403 employed U.S. Christians.

LET'S TALK ABOUT ... THE RELATIONAL ASPECTS OF VOCATION

❝ If you look back, even in the Old Testament, relationships—specifically covenantal, Trinitarian relationships—are the precedent for creativity. It comes before God's creation of the world. I think that relationships are so crucial to how we figure out where we're headed next. That happens often in educational settings. It happens among peers. It happens in families. We can have it embedded in the larger mission of the Church."

—Michaela O'Donnell Long, PhD, senior director of Max De Pree Center for Leadership, owner of Long Winter Media

Generations, Vocations and Church Engagement

◆ Millennials ◆ Gen X ◆ Boomers

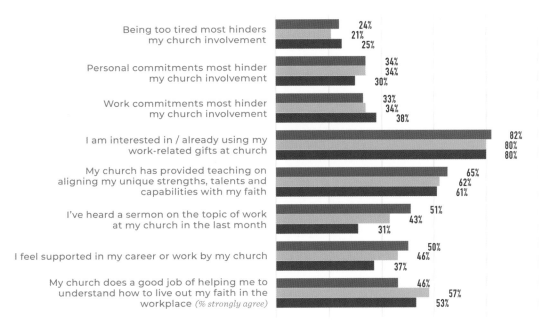

Being too tired most hinders
my church involvement — 24% / 21% / 25%

Personal commitments most hinder
my church involvement — 34% / 34% / 30%

Work commitments most hinder
my church involvement — 33% / 34% / 38%

I am interested in / already using my
work-related gifts at church — 82% / 80% / 80%

My church has provided teaching on
aligning my unique strengths, talents and
capabilities with my faith — 65% / 62% / 61%

I've heard a sermon on the topic of work
at my church in the last month — 51% / 43% / 31%

I feel supported in my career or work by my church — 50% / 46% / 37%

My church does a good job of helping me to
understand how to live out my faith in the
workplace *(% strongly agree)* — 46% / 57% / 53%

n=701 employed U.S. Christians who attend church monthly.

❝ Mentors that have been especially influential in my life are those who have veered me back to myself, my passions and skills and have even given negative feedback when necessary. They've also made things happen; for example, one mentor helped me write my first book proposal. I encourage younger folks to seek out mentors who can clearly see them for who they are—the good, bad and maybe ugly—but who will also go to the effort to open doors."

—*Dr. Pamela Ebstyne King, author, professor at the Thrive Center at Fuller Theological Seminary*

Conversations with Practitioners

presence in the marketplace.

Just beyond Millennials is Gen Z, and it remains to be seen what kind of long-term engagement they may have with the Church at all. Currently, Barna finds, they primarily define themselves by academic or career success, with faith and family further down the list. This distinguishes them from other generations, including their parents, who might need some help in grounding the ambitions of their teens: One in four engaged Christian parents (24%) has talked with their son or daughter in the past year about integrating faith in their future career, and one-third of parents whose child attends church (34%) says addressing vocation is an area in which the youth program is weakest. It will be a significant and pivotal undertaking for churches to help these emerging adults become more vocationally minded than career-oriented.

PASTORS' EXPERIENCES & VIEWS
OF VOCATION

Overall, pastors appear well-positioned as leaders on the subject of vocation, and they think their churches are successful in equipping congregants to discuss religion or faith at work (71%). The pastors who take vocational discipleship seriously, through their church programs as well as their personal connections, play a vital role in preparing Christians to faithfully engage with their daily lives and workplaces, as well as shaping those called to a future in ministry themselves.

Most pastors first felt a calling to ministry in their teen or early adult years, but that doesn't mean they took a fast track to the clergy. More than half (55%) had another career before going into ministry. Roughly one-quarter (26%) remains bivocational, currently holding some other kind of (paid or unpaid) role in addition to pastoring, usually for non-financial motivations like personal fulfillment or having other outlets for their gifts.

Though over one-third of pastors (36%) admits occasionally wishing for another calling, responses suggest that ministry suits these leaders well. A majority feels content (72%) and is very satisfied with their opportunity to use their spiritual gifts (81%) or talents (77%) as a pastor. Sixty-two percent are very confident in the preparation they are receiving for their future. They also think their educational background—including seminary, for three-quarters of pastors (76%)—is a good fit

Pastors' Career Experiences

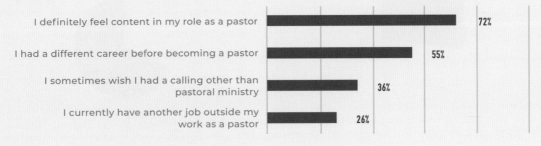

- I definitely feel content in my role as a pastor — 72%
- I had a different career before becoming a pastor — 55%
- I sometimes wish I had a calling other than pastoral ministry — 36%
- I currently have another job outside my work as a pastor — 26%

n=424 U.S. pastors.

for their role (78%). Nearly two-thirds (64%) see at least a possibility of pursuing additional education, including one-third (33%) who is already doing so.

How do pastors believe churches should address vocation, whether from the pulpit or in programs? Nearly two-fifths of pastors (38%) view faith communities as "essential" in helping Christians identify their own strengths and capabilities. They say this should be prioritized through sermons (86%), classes and tests (85%) or small groups (83%). Most seem to be following through: Pastors report that the topic of vocation has come up in their preaching in the past couple years (79%), often multiple

times (49% say five or more times in the past two years). Indeed, as a comparison, roughly four in 10 Christian workers Barna surveyed (42%) have heard a message about work from their church in the past month.

Still, there could be some missed opportunities to reach the churchgoers most likely to be in the midst of career development; few pastors report providing designated ministries or programs for singles or college students, and mentorship programs aren't very common church offerings (20%). The majority of pastors, however, says they *personally* have a mentee, either in ministry (74%) or another industry (68%).

Read more about senior pastors' experiences of calling, as well as their personal, relational and spiritual well-being, in Barna's *The State of Pastors* report.

Most Pastors Mentor Someone Else

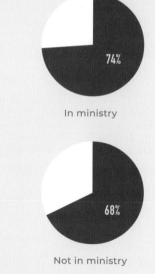

74%

In ministry

68%

Not in ministry

n=424 U.S. pastors.

A BIVOCATIONAL VISION OF MINISTRY

A Q&A with Sam Whitehawk

Q In this survey, Barna asked respondents if it's better to become a pastor or missionary or to represent one's faith well at work. As a bivocational leader, how would you answer this question? And how would you encourage Christians to recognize the spiritual nature and value of their employment—blue-collar, white-collar, pink-collar and so on?

A When I initially left Bible college and entered into bivocational ministry, I struggled with the belief that full-time vocational ministry was how you truly made a difference. It took a few years into my career to realize that God uses believers in the marketplace to do this, too. Now, after 10 years of bivocational work, I can faithfully answer that neither is better than the other. As God builds his Church, he will use many different vocation options to reach unbelievers.

I would encourage believers to recognize that, as Spirit-filled followers of Christ, they are ambassadors wherever they are in their employment. The Great Commission calls us to make disciples, and this is possible whether they are pastors, missionaries or working in the marketplace.

Q What is your advice to those who experience work as a "daily grind" and struggle to integrate their faith and their work?

A I experienced this early in my career as I struggled with whether I had made the right decision to enter into construction instead of full-time youth or college ministry. The work was not glamorous or rewarding. What helped change my perspective, however, was knowing I was building relationships with men I would never otherwise meet and get to speak to every day. I would let them know I was a Christian right away and let them work through their misconceptions while sharing with them the gospel.

My advice is for men and women to work hard and represent Christ well. And by revealing they are Christian as soon as possible, they allow people to see how Christ transforms someone's life and perspective of work. The other advice I offer to people is to regularly pray for their coworkers and work to build relationship outside of work.

Q How do you think each of your bivocational roles informs or enhances the other in your community?

A It is very important for me to remain bivocational because God has given me a calling to reach unbelievers in our city. We have found that those who we are trying to reach respect and trust those who show their work ethic in the workplace, but there seems to be mistrust of those who are in full-time ministry. As an indigenous man, I have been very fortunate to have built a career that has led me to now work for an indigenous school with a very wide reach in our province. This role has allowed me to gain influence with many people and community leaders whom I could never reach otherwise. Having this other role allows me to disciple and evangelize with an understanding of what our people are going through on a daily basis. When we design discipleship systems and events, I always keep in mind people like me who work 40 hours a week outside the church and home, so I know our time is limited.

SAM WHITEHAWK
Pastor

Whitehawk is one of the bivocational pastors at Grace Fellowship in Saskatoon, Saskatchewan, Canada. He is a journeyperson electrician with eight years of experience in the trade, including three years as an electrical supervisor. He is currently a program coordinator for an indigenous institute that specializes in training men and women for employment. He and his wife, Allison, have been married since 2009 and have three wonderful daughters. Whitehawk is being sent out as the lead church planter in their community of Evergreen, Saskatoon, in 2019.

Q How can churches help those with the most positive vocational experiences to avoid burnout and steward their skills and influence well? On the other hand, how can they make sure that some of the groups who are less engaged in church or who experience less vocational support from the church are still being discipled in this way?

A I think that having small groups with different schedules and diversified ages and skills will help everyone be engaged in serving. I believe that churches should be mindful of planning small groups around those with varying schedules, ensuring that those who have different workloads are still able to encourage and be encouraged. Being in community and being given opportunities to serve in roles that suit their schedules prevents burnout. It requires those with more flexibility to be intentional about making those who are busier feel included. And it requires pastors who oversee them to be intentional about reaching those on the fringes. This type of discipleship will help grow a healthy church. This is something we focus on as a church, and it has been helpful in getting more people in community.

"Having this other role allows me to disciple and evangelize with an understanding of what our people are going through on a daily basis."

THE PRACTICING FAITH BONUS

Workers who consistently attend church and highly value their personal faith have purposeful and rewarding vocational experiences

- ◆ Practicing Christians
- ◆ Non-practicing Christians

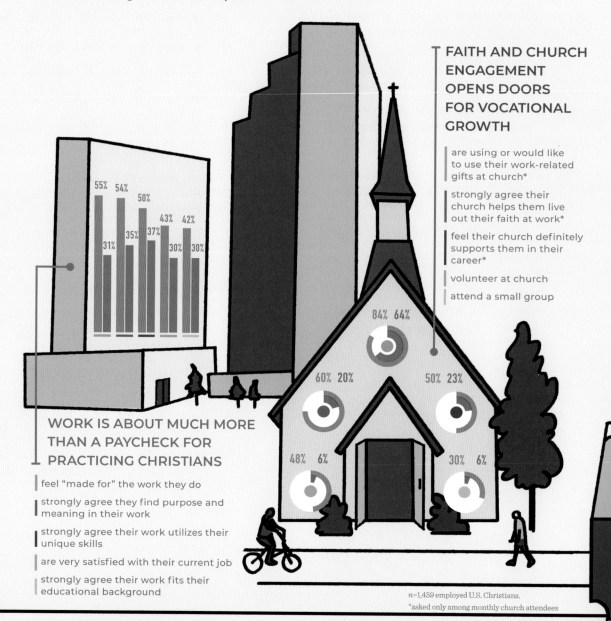

FAITH AND CHURCH ENGAGEMENT OPENS DOORS FOR VOCATIONAL GROWTH

84% 64%
are using or would like to use their work-related gifts at church*

60% 20%
strongly agree their church helps them live out their faith at work*

50% 23%
feel their church definitely supports them in their career*

48% 6%
volunteer at church

30% 6%
attend a small group

WORK IS ABOUT MUCH MORE THAN A PAYCHECK FOR PRACTICING CHRISTIANS

- 55% 31% — feel "made for" the work they do
- 54% 35% — strongly agree they find purpose and meaning in their work
- 50% 37% — strongly agree their work utilizes their unique skills
- 43% 30% — are very satisfied with their current job
- 42% 30% — strongly agree their work fits their educational background

n=1,459 employed U.S. Christians.
*asked only among monthly church attendees

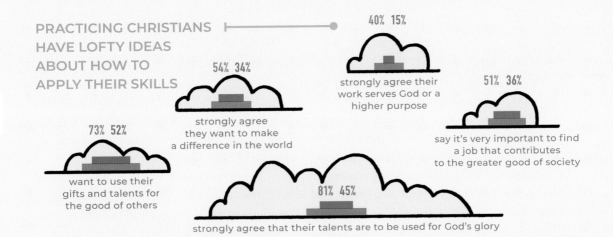

PRACTICING CHRISTIANS HAVE LOFTY IDEAS ABOUT HOW TO APPLY THEIR SKILLS

40% 15% strongly agree their work serves God or a higher purpose

54% 34% strongly agree they want to make a difference in the world

51% 36% say it's very important to find a job that contributes to the greater good of society

73% 52% want to use their gifts and talents for the good of others

81% 45% strongly agree that their talents are to be used for God's glory

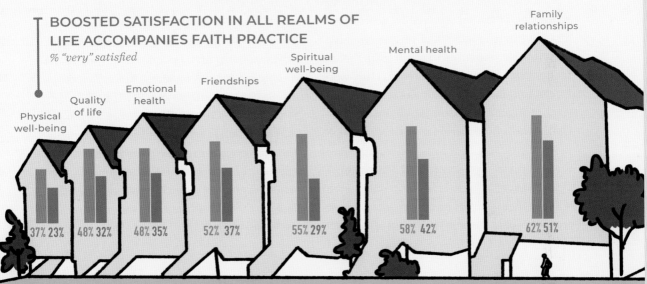

BOOSTED SATISFACTION IN ALL REALMS OF LIFE ACCOMPANIES FAITH PRACTICE

% "very" satisfied

Physical well-being **37% 23%**

Quality of life **48% 32%**

Emotional health **48% 35%**

Friendships **52% 37%**

Spiritual well-being **55% 29%**

Mental health **58% 42%**

Family relationships **62% 51%**

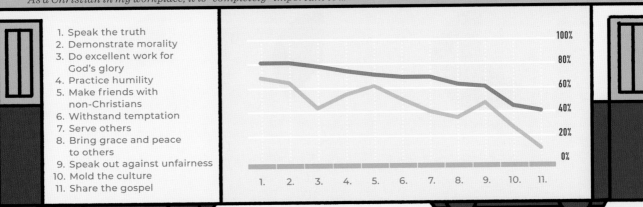

PRACTICING CHRISTIANS BRING HIGH STANDARDS INTO THE MARKETPLACE

As a Christian in my workplace, it is "completely" important to ...

1. Speak the truth
2. Demonstrate morality
3. Do excellent work for God's glory
4. Practice humility
5. Make friends with non-Christians
6. Withstand temptation
7. Serve others
8. Bring grace and peace to others
9. Speak out against unfairness
10. Mold the culture
11. Share the gospel

DISCIPLING EVERY CHRISTIAN WORKER

Integrators may be exceptional models for centering faith and finding purpose in the workplace, but keep in mind that they are a minority. While there is a lot of good news to share about how all Christians are professionally engaging their vocation, Barna wanted to take a closer look at the motivations and, at times, limitations of those who don't qualify as Integrators of faith and work.

As mentioned, Barna determined the categories of Christian workers by scoring and grouping individuals based on the combination of their responses to some telling statements about vocation and career. If faith-work Integrators are those who show the highest level of agreement, **Compartmentalizers**—Christians who experience their work separately from faith or a sense of calling—have a low level of agreement, and **Onlookers**—Christians who have a passive interest in aligning their calling and career—have a moderate level of agreement with these ideas. Each

of these two groups represents more than a third of Barna's sample of working Christians (Onlookers 38%, Compartmentalizers 34%). (Refer to page 50 for a breakdown of Barna's metric of faith-work integration.)

There are some ways in which Compartmentalizers and Onlookers are similar to each other, in that they are simply other than Integrators. For example, neither group is quite as ambitious (67% of Integrators, 43% of Onlookers and 44% of Compartmentalizers say it's very important to find opportunities for advancement) and, by definition, they aren't as concerned with making a difference in the world (91% of Integrators, 21% of Onlookers and 23% of Compartmentalizers "strongly" agree). Yet on other points, these two non-Integrator groups diverge, representing a true spectrum of vocational engagement. The nuances may provide keys for churches that hope to thoughtfully nurture the spiritual and professional fulfillment of all in their services.

Percentage of Practicing Christians Across Vocational Profiles

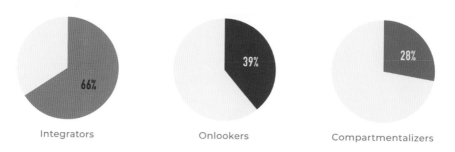

Integrators — 66%

Onlookers — 39%

Compartmentalizers — 28%

n=1,459 employed U.S. Christians.

Although, for some of these workers, attending church is a rare occasion to begin with: Practicing faith decreases as you move from Integrators to Compartmentalizers.

When Work & Faith Are Insulated

Just one in 10 Compartmentalizers (11% vs. 77% of Integrators) feels called to or made for their current work. Even more revealing: One in five Compartmentalizers (22%) says they have never even thought about whether their calling and career overlap (vs. 6% of Integrators). A similar proportion among the Compartmentalizers (23%) does not find use for their work-related gifts outside the office. This is one peek into Compartmentalizers' pragmatic, utilitarian approach to career. It'd be unfair to assume they don't care about their gifts or purpose—44 percent still strongly agree they possess God-given abilities—but it is perhaps accurate to say that their other concerns take precedence over considering how those gifts are utilized in a 9-to-5.

The most defining factor in Compartmentalizers' identity is "family" (48%), which sets them apart from both Integrators and Onlookers, who are more likely to see "faith" as central to their sense of self. Accordingly, Compartmentalizers' ultimate financial goals are typically focused

---

One in four Compartmentalizers says they have never even thought about whether their calling and career overlap

---

Spirit, Soul *and* Body: Physical Well-being in Vocation

At the end of the day, Integrators, Onlookers and Compartmentalizers are just human—which is something that all Christian workers could use a reminder of. Across the board, regardless of age, gender, stage of life, status or vocational personality, **physical well-being is the area of life consistently ranked lowest in terms of satisfaction**. In recent years, there has been no shortage of alarming headlines about the health risks of sitting on the job,[51] and many workers know firsthand the side effects of stress, from headaches to heart disease.[52] Still, taking care of oneself also takes time—which, as Barna's report shows at several points, many Christian workers are hard-pressed to find. But in embodying one's calling, the "body" can't be neglected. Plenty of workplaces are getting creative about encouraging employees to move, take breaks and practice self-care. Churches helping their members navigate work-life balance could take some cues from these companies as they consider vocational discipleship programs. If vocation is about infusing meaning into daily tasks, that should include meals, walks, time in nature and, that discipline so often mandated in scripture, rest.

Awareness of and Utilization of Calling

◆ Integrators   ◆ Onlookers   ◆ Compartmentalizers

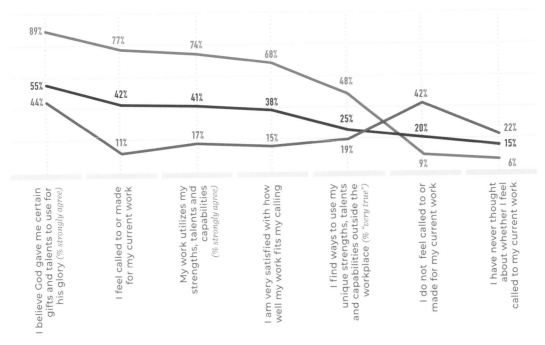

n=1,459 employed U.S. Christians.

on providing for their family (61%), as well as meeting obligations and needs (46%) or achieving the lifestyle they want (37%). Some of this could be related to the fact that Compartmentalizer parents are the most likely to have young children at home. Serving God with money, however, is much less of a priority (20% vs. 45% of Integrators). Compartmentalizers are largely middle-class, yet most often describe their financial status as stable but making ends meet (39%).

Generally, Compartmentalizers seem to concentrate on what they can earn, rather than spiritually contribute, in employment. The issue is not that Compartmentalizers—the most notionally Christian group (49%)—already have a robust faith that is kept out of their work, but that they aren't very spiritually active in general (despite their affirmation that faith is important to them on some level). Thus, they don't see urgency in impacting the workplace based on religious convictions. At times, they're even quite averse to it: Six in 10 say it's unimportant to share

Satisfaction in Life and Work
% very satisfied with the following

◆ Integrators   ◆ Onlookers   ◆ Compartmentalizers

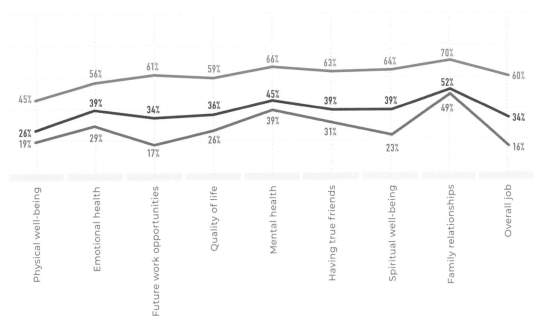

n=1,459 employed U.S. Christians

the gospel as an employee (30% "not at all" + 29% "not very"), while majorities of both Onlookers (42% "somewhat" + 18% "completely") and Integrators (35% "somewhat" + 44% "completely") call this an opportunity for Christians.

Even among churched respondents, few Compartmentalizers are using their work-related gifts at church (23%)—in fact, a third (33%) is not even interested in doing so. These attendees also rarely report that their church supports them in their career (23%

"definitely") or addresses vocation (27% have heard a related sermon in the past month, 56% say their church provides related resources). The researchers can't discern from this study alone whether Compartmentalizers experience less vocational stimulation from the Church as a result of their own indifference or because of an actual lack of church resources that meet their needs—but it's clear there is a disconnect between these Christian workers and their faith communities.

The profile of Compartmentalizers is

often one of family men and women, striving most for stability. Their world is divided into stark categories: professional and personal, external and internal, physical and spiritual. On paper, it's a balanced, even logical approach—and in some life circumstances or events that require it, it may be. But in Barna's survey results, neither realm of life (nor the Compartmentalizer as a whole person) seems to benefit from the separation: This group is the least satisfied with the overall quality of their life (26% "very" satisfied) and work (16%), especially with their future prospects (17%), friendships (31%) and emotional (29%), spiritual (23%) or physical (19%) well-being.

When Vocation Becomes a Spectator Sport

Throughout the survey, Onlookers speak loudest in what they do not assert: They tend to offer middling responses, favoring "somewhat" over "definitely." These are the workers willing to take only minor risks (52%) and only

moderately interested in the world around them (38% "strongly" agree). Their satisfaction levels in turn track down the middle, whether in their work overall (34% "very" satisfied), their relationships with family (52%) and friends (39%) or their mental (45%), spiritual (39%) and emotional (39%) health.

You could think of Onlookers as apathetic or stagnant, or as potential Integrators whose vocational passion has not yet been refined or released. From the data emerges a portrait of an ambivalent yet well-meaning group who could be compelled to act on a healthy interest in improving themselves (54% "strongly" + 43% "somewhat" agree), making a difference (21% "strongly" + 70% "somewhat" agree) and using their talents for the good of others (59% "strongly" + 40% "somewhat" agree) or for God's glory (55% "strongly" + 41% "somewhat" agree). And though you couldn't characterize Onlookers as overly eager to shape the culture of their workplace (20% "completely" important), this is something they could be spurred

---

LET'S TALK ABOUT ... STEPPING INTO A CALLING

66 Sometimes there's a lot of inertia. You feel you have the call, but you're waiting for that perfect moment to step into the call. And I don't think life works that way. I think you just have to move."

—Sheeba Philip, marketing executive for global brands and non-profits

66 Even when we talk about talents and gifts, we often discount any hard work that we have to do to get there. I would actually say calling is a co-activity between the Lord giving us certain things and us actually developing them as well."

—Bethany Jenkins, vice president of forums for The Veritas Forum

toward, as 58 percent still call it "somewhat" important. As a whole, their responses suggest good intentions and latent gifts.

Onlookers aspire to a more meaningful connection not only with their daily work, but also with their local church. While one in three Onlookers who attend church monthly (32%) uses their work-related gifts to serve there, 47 percent are open to it. More than a third of the churched in this group (34% "strongly") is confident in the professional support they receive from their church, which they say includes vocation-related sermons (12% weekly + 25% monthly) and other resources (55%).

Psychological assessments of calling say it is realized in both perceiving *and* enacting a sense of purpose.[53] So it's unfortunate that Onlookers and Compartmentalizers seem to be stuck on the first part of that process. One of the biggest barriers for each of these vocational personalities, and one of the more obvious gaps between them and Integrators, is that they are unsure of their calling to begin with. Two-thirds of Integrators (66%) agree strongly that they are aware of their God-given gifts and talents; they are joined by just 33 percent of Onlookers and 24 percent of Compartmentalizers. For these Christians, the first question to be answered isn't "How am I molding my workplace?" or "What company am I called to lead or start?" Rather, it might be more pertinent to begin with: "How am I uniquely wired?" "What are the skills and capabilities God has granted me?" "How can I imbue my day-to-day work with deeper meaning and a spiritual awareness?"

> Onlookers aspire to a more meaningful connection not only with their daily work, but also with their local church

---

❝ If you live your life, and you're waiting and hoping for this amazing passion to emerge, that's very unlikely to happen. Good research shows that passion emerges from trying and doing stuff, reflecting on it and learning about yourself. ... It's a minority of people who are crystal clear."

—Michaela O'Donnell Long, PhD, senior director of Max De Pree Center for Leadership, owner of Long Winter Media

Conversations with Practitioners

Vocational Connections to the Church
% among monthly church attendees

◆ Integrators   ◆ Onlookers   ◆ Compartmentalizers

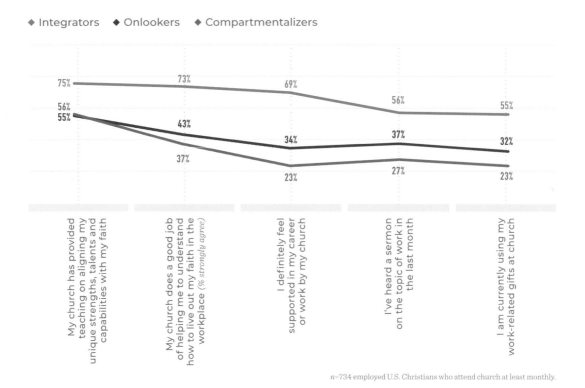

75%   73%   69%   56%   55%
56%
55%   43%   34%   37%   32%
      37%   23%   27%   23%

My church has provided teaching on aligning my unique strengths, talents and capabilities with my faith

My church does a good job of helping me to understand how to live out my faith in the workplace *(% strongly agree)*

I definitely feel supported in my career or work by my church

I've heard a sermon on the topic of work in the last month

I am currently using my work-related gifts at church

n=734 employed U.S. Christians who attend church at least monthly.

This is not to say that Integrators of faith and work have it all figured out or are somehow not in need of vocational direction from the Church. Though their reported ideals are admirable, other research shows optimism alone doesn't always translate to productive actions or commitments for the long term.[54] Some Integrators may also be at risk of being misguided by their own lofty ambitions—after all, this is the segment most likely to anticipate that their career could put them in charge or make them famous. As Mark Labberton writes,

"From a Kingdom perspective, vocation isn't primarily about how to find fulfillment and satisfaction. The frequent assumption is that we seek to find the perfect way to get the most out of life as the unique and wonderful people we are. That's more a reflection of narcissism than healthy self-esteem, let alone Christlike humility and servanthood. There will be joy in our call, but that is different from making the pursuit of happiness our priority."[55] Further, as we noted earlier in this chapter, though Integrators are the most engaged with the

Church, a significant proportion of them points to work commitments as an obstacle to their church involvement. Theirs is a temperament of extremes, capable of burning bright or burning out.

Vocational discipleship is not one-size-fits-all, just as every Christian, every home, every job is not the same. There are many extenuating reasons and seasons that influence an employee's relationship to their calling through their job. But in generally assessing these three groups, and in hoping every believer might work earnestly and for God's glory, the opportunity for the Church is:

- to help Compartmentalizers connect with their faith and recognize the sacred value of their work,
- to help Onlookers move in from the sidelines and be active participants in their callings
- and to help Integrators steward their influence and share their passion.

One of the biggest vocational barriers for both Onlookers and Compartmentalizers is that they are unsure of their calling to begin with

REST WELL, WORK WELL

BY ROXANNE STONE

When presented with a list of life activities, do you know what the majority of people identifies as their top desire?

A good night's rest.

More than exotic travel, fancy restaurants, concerts, hanging out with friends—people just really want to get some sleep.[56] At least, that's what adults told Barna in 2006—and we can probably all agree things haven't exactly gotten *less* stressful in the years since.

In a separate Barna survey, 53 percent of adults admit to having felt physically or mentally overwhelmed in the past month. Less than half of adults profess to feeling satisfaction in any of the following areas: work-life balance, overall rest, relationship boundaries and overall stress. And 71 percent say they feel overwhelmed by information.[57]

What does it mean to live in a sleep-deprived, always stressed and digitally distracted society?

Well, among other things, it means the economy has won out over spirituality.

While work is often a rewarding and purpose-filled endeavor, God's intention was never that it superseded all other aspects of our life. No matter how you answer that familiar question, "Do you live to work or work to live?" a healthy and holistic life requires more than work. This is particularly true when it comes to our spiritual health. Spirituality requires presence, mindfulness, contemplation, observation. Spirituality rarely happens in the margins of our schedules. And who among us today even has any margin?

Have you ever read *Pilgrim at Tinker Creek*? This Pulitzer prize-winning memoir is nothing if not a celebration of the ordinary, sl"ow-lived life—and the beauty encoun-

"What does it mean to live in a sleep-deprived, always stressed and digitally distracted society? It means the economy has won out over spirituality."

tered there. Annie Dillard writes of the most banal things: a river's quickening, a tadpole in the mud, the changing of seasons along one streambed. She spends hours and hours wandering her woods: praying, observing, contemplating.

Do you make time to wander the woods? Or to sit in a subway without your headphones in or a screen in front of you and instead peer into the faces of your fellow travelers—to wonder about and observe the lives playing out around you?

If you are serious about your faith and your spiritual health, you must make time for it. And not just for the practical disciplines of it, but for the blossoming of it. The blossoming that comes from rest, from emptying your mind of your to-do list and your jammed inbox, from wandering and wondering and observing both your own inner life and the world around you.

In her acclaimed workbook *The Artist's Way*, Julia Cameron insists on two weekly tasks that are entirely non-negotiable for the artist (and neither of which have anything to do with creating art): writing three pages of longhand first thing every morning to clear your head, and taking your "artist" on a date (with no one else present) once a week. These are rituals of rest and replenishment. Such rituals are not just helpful for those of us who are artists. They are helpful for anyone who is trying to cultivate a rich spiritual life—who is seeking to infuse the rest of their everyday life and work with the wisdom, empathy, curiosity and imagination that stems from a deep faith. The study for this report alone clearly and repeatedly shows how deep faith is connected to—perhaps even a determinant of—fulfilling vocational experiences.

Work will always be a central part of the human life. We long for meaning and purpose and we find great pleasure in a job well done. We will always find ourselves with more work to be done. But, like a marathon runner carbo-loading before a race, your inner life must be nourished. An underfed runner will not finish the race. An underfed faith will give you a starved spirituality.

Enter the fourth commandment. Those

ROXANNE STONE is editor in chief at Barna Group. She is the former editorial director for *RELEVANT* magazine and has worked in publishing for more than 15 years, serving as an editor at *Christianity Today*, Group Publishing, Q Ideas and This is Our City. She is currently working on a book examining healthy relationships between men and women in every realm of life. You can follow her on Twitter at @roxyleestone.

of us who follow the God of the Old and New Testament should have an advantage here, when it comes to rest. We are commanded to do so: to take one day a week for a Sabbath. However, while we are quick to reaffirm the other nine commandments, we get a little squishy around that one. *A whole day? What does it mean not to work? What if I get an urgent email on a Sunday?* Taking a whole day off just doesn't really fly in our uber-productive day and age. Yet, God didn't equivocate on this. In fact, he commanded, *"Above all,* keep my Sabbaths ... there are six days for work but the seventh day is Sabbath, pure rest, holy to God" (Exodus 31:12, 14, *The Message,* emphasis added). Above all the other commands, the Israelites were to obey the Sabbath. This is the command that set them apart from the culture around them.

We know from our research at Barna that the vast majority of people, including Christians, does not take a Sabbath. And when they do, the most common activity they indulge in on that day is "enjoyable work." Call it Puritan work ethic or Christian pragmatism, but rest is just not something we do well. Even the faith-work Integrators identified in this report, for all of their admirable vocational attitudes, show signs of being prone to overworking, or at least over-identifying with productivity and accomplishment.

There is money to make and jobs to do and errands to run and children to feed, of course. Time, it seems, is in ever-short supply. But, in this case, the old adage rings true: "If you ignore it, it will go away." If you ignore your spirituality, it will go away. Or, rather, your interior world will wither and die. So take the time. Intentionally carve out an hour a day, a day a week, maybe a weekend a quarter and a week a year for God—for your faith. Enjoy a book, listen to some music, read some poetry, take a long walk, go to church and worship your Creator who has infused you with his creativity.

Bless yourself with rest and you will be able to bless the world with your work.

CONCLUSION

The Next Phase of Vocational Discipleship

There are two economies in our world, according to novelist and farmer Wendell Berry—a "little" or human economy, and a Great Economy, which Christians understand as the Kingdom of God.[58] "Work that is authentically placed and understood within the Great Economy moves virtue toward virtuosity—that is, toward skill or technical competence," he writes. "There is no use in helping our neighbors with their work if we do not know how to work. When the virtues are rightly practiced within the Great Economy, we do not call them virtues; we call them good farming, good forestry, good carpentry, good husbandry, good weaving and sewing, good homemaking, good parenthood, good neighborhood and so on."

This report aims to point to the place where these two economies overlap. And our vision is that church leaders, as individuals whose own calling is to know and share the values of the Great Economy, might encourage others to move through the human economy virtuously and with an awareness of the spiritual underpinnings of their profession.

Through this study alone, we don't get a glimpse of people's daily commutes, conference calls and to-do lists. We don't know which Christian workers actually receive good performance reviews or have strong rapport with colleagues. We can't deduce the exact and best way for a pastor or mentor to produce a transformative vocational outlook in, say, a stockbroker, guidance counselor, line cook, rideshare driver or freelance photographer. But the objective with any Barna project is that the general observations from our data will be filtered through the vivid lens of your personal

experience and influence—that our findings would have some impact on your doings.

What we *do* glean from this study is that Christians who seek to be genuine, faithful, curious and helpful in their working lives also report being generally more satisfied with the whole of their lives. And we see that the consistent tending of one's relationship with God and with the Church is conducive to all of the above. In looking at the Integrators of faith and work and the responses in our practitioner interviews, we encounter an undeniable zeal for learning more, taking risks, serving God and making an impact that dispels any sense of work as drudgery.

But the data also reveals some disparities and deficiencies. The majority of Christian workers, particularly those who aren't engaged in a church, still fights to discern and act on a calling in their professional lives. Studying responses by gender is like watching a vocational seesaw, with women thriving during singlehood and men thriving during fatherhood. Young adults, though ambitious and idealistic, lack some spiritual inclinations as workers. Older adults, with one foot out the door of the workplace, might need some encouragement to finish strong.

Our prayer is that, as these themes unfold in the data, you feel prompted to specifically and practically develop a strategy for the integration of faith and work in your congregation, class, program or team, as well as in your own life. To help you in that effort, Barna has come up with some constructive questions to serve you as a minister and a "crossing guard" of sorts at the intersection of calling and career.

Raising up

These questions are intended to help church leaders identify, equip and develop all Christians to have an intentional, Kingdom-oriented view of their vocation.

◆ In reviewing the spectrum of vocational personalities (page 50), do you recognize people with whom you interact or exercise influence? If so, who are the Integrators who need to be championed and anchored in their growth? Who are the Onlookers who need to be nudged (or even pushed) to embrace their calling in work? Who are the Compartmentalizers—most likely notional Christians at the fringes of your faith community—who could be welcomed in to hear the truth that they are chosen and called?

- How do your ministries provide opportunities for people with seemingly less pastoral roles or skill sets to worship or lead out of their strengths? How can your church become more shaped and led by workers of various backgrounds and industries? What does the "priesthood of all believers" look like today, and how do you mobilize people around that vision?

- What does it entail to help women and men approach each professional and relational season of their lives with purpose? In terms of location, scheduling, content or format, are your services, programs or small groups accessible to working individuals in all stages of life? How is your church, as members of the family of God, watching out for the vocational needs of the families in your congregation and speaking to mothers and fathers as partners in vocation—at home and work?

- Has your church ever gone through assessments, devotional plans, sermon series or seasons of prayer and fasting with the sole intent of helping people identify their God-given callings—not just spiritual gifts, but general or vocational strengths, abilities and motivations?

- Does your church have a formal plan for reaching younger adults in a career-building stage? How often does your youth ministry tackle the topic of the spiritual nature of work, especially with the success-oriented Gen Z who currently occupy youth groups? Are you effectively connecting people in multigenerational mentorships—which could be one way to engage and learn from experienced Boomers in the latter stages of career?

Looking inward

These questions are intended to inspire reflection or instruction on the spiritual principles and motivations of our working lives.

- Have you ever (even unintentionally) reinforced the idea of a hierarchy of professions or of "sacred vs. secular" work? In your private study and your public sermons or statements, how are you cultivating a broader imagination for what it looks like to participate in the Kingdom of God?

- In talking about work, how often do you talk about rest? Do your staff policies lead by example, challenging a culture that glorifies hustle at the expense of well-being, spiritual growth, sabbath or free time?

- How can you help workers take a contemplative or prayerful stance in their daily routines, whether they are on the morning train, meeting a customer or signing a contract? Do you ever speak of spiritual disciplines as job skills?

◆ What does scripture really have to say about work? As Jo Saxton mentions on page 42, are we taking note of the jobs we see represented by biblical figures, as well as the vocational lessons they impart? How often do your messages focus on these themes?

◆ How can you encourage vocation as an act of incarnation in a post-Christian era? As working lives are increasingly digital and potentially disconnected, where are the opportunities to recognize personhood and affirm the *imago Dei,* even in the marketplace?

Reaching out

These questions are intended to frame vocational discipleship as a crucial missional opportunity, not a secondary focus.

◆ How could vocational instruction help skeptical younger generations see faith as relevant to their lives?

◆ What are the industries represented most in your community and your church? What unique challenges do workers in these fields face when it comes to relational, financial, spiritual or physical well-being? Could your ministry love your neighbors through vocationally oriented "community service"—practical seminars, meals, supply drives, coffee & prayer gatherings and so on?

◆ Who are the local educators, managers, business leaders and entrepreneurs your church can partner with to develop a comprehensive vocational vision that meets the needs of employees and businesses in your community?

◆ Rather than only drawing people to your church, who are the workers and leaders who already sit in your services and are ready to be sent out? What are you doing to equip them to, as Dr. Ben Ries writes on page 66, represent the Kingdom coming near—to bridge the little economy and Great Economy?

As you digest the data in this report and prayerfully ask these questions, we hope you find answers that invigorate you in your own calling and sustain your church as a partner in God's redemptive work in the world.

METHODOLOGY

This study began with qualitative interviews of 33 practitioners and thought leaders, representing a range of industries, conducted in December 2017 and January 2018. These phone interviews used a flexible script exploring respondents' experiences of faith and work.

Subsequently, a set of quantitative online surveys was conducted February 27–March 12, 2018, and April 18–May 8, 2018, using an online panel. The sample included 1,459 self-identified U.S. Christians who agree somewhat or strongly that their faith is very important in their life today and are employed (full-time, part-time or self-employed, including unpaid work for a family business). The margin of error for this sample is +/- 2.3 percent at the 95 percent confidence level.

All research that seeks to capture the dynamics of a population has some inherent limitations, but is useful to observe patterns and differences that reveal insights about the surveyed group. Online panels are a collection of people who have pre-agreed to take surveys for some compensation, which may represent some motivational biases, so our surveys include quality control measures to ensure respondents are providing truthful and thoughtful answers to questions. When Barna samples from panels, respondents are invited from a randomly selected group of people matching the demographics of the U.S. population for maximum representation. For this study, our researchers set quotas to obtain a minimum readable sample by a variety of demographic factors and weighted the data by ethnicity, education and gender to reflect

Working Christians

Generation	Millennial 29%	Gen X 41%	Boomer 27%	Elder 2%
Ethnicity*	White 72%	African American / Black 14%	Latino / Hispanic 13%	Asian 4%
Relationship Status	Married 57%	Single 27%	Divorced / separated / widowed 16%	
Children	Children under 18 living in their home 37%			
Education	High school or less 18%	Some higher education** 48%	Bachelor's degree 22%	Graduate degree 12%
Work	Full-time 73%	Part-time 17%	Self-employed 10%	
Total Household Income	Less than $50K 36%	$50K–$99K 44%	$100K+ 20%	

*respondents could select multiple ethnicities

**including associate's or technical degree

their natural presence in the working population (using U.S. Census Bureau and Bureau of Labor Statistics data for comparison). Partly by nature of using an online panel and partly due to focusing only on the employed population, these respondents are slightly more educated and higher earning than the average American. Also, due to the natural makeup of the practicing Christian population, the proportion of black adults is greater than Hispanic adults in this sample when compared to the general American population.

Another quantitative online survey of 424 U.S. Protestant senior pastors was conducted March 1–March 12, 2018. These pastors were recruited from Barna's pastor panel (a database of pastors recruited via probability sampling on annual phone and email surveys) and are representative of U.S. Protestant churches by region, denomination and church size. The margin of error for this sample is +/- 4.8 percent at the 95 percent confidence level.

GLOSSARY

Generation
Gen Z: born between 1999 and 2015
Millennials: born between 1984 and 1998
Gen X: born between 1965 and 1983
Boomers: born between 1946 and 1964
Elders: born between 1945 or earlier

The spectrum of **faith & work integration** (Integrators, Onlookers and Compartmentalizers) was defined based on a cluster analysis of the following statements:

- "I can clearly see how the work that I am doing is serving God or a higher purpose."
- "I find purpose and meaning in the work I do."
- "I am looking to make a difference in the world."
- "As a Christian in my workplace, I believe it is important to help mold the culture of my workplace."

Entrepreneurial Integrators are categorized as Integrators based on the above, and are also open to taking risks and starting their own business.

Practicing Christians are self-identified Christians who say their faith is very important in their lives and have attended a worship service within the past month.

Churched respondents have attended a worship service within the past six months.

NOTES

1. Anahad O'Connor, "The Claim: Heart Attacks Are More Common on Mondays," *New York Times,* March 14, 2006. https://www.nytimes.com/2006/03/14/health/14real.html. Uppsala University, "Less Myocardial Infarctions During Summer Vacation—More on Mondays and Winter Holidays," July 6, 2017. https://www.eurekalert.org/pub_releases/2017-07/uu-lmi070617.php.

2. Jim Clifton, *The Coming Jobs War* (Gallup Press, 2011), 8-11.

3. Steven Garber, *Visions of Vocation: Common Grace for the Common Good* (Intervarsity Press, 2014).

4. Jenna Goudreau, "Find Happiness at Work," *Forbes,* https://www.forbes.com/2010/03/04/happiness-work-resilience-forbes-woman-well-being-satisfaction.html#25afb8ab126a.

5. David Kinnaman, *You Lost Me: Why Young Christians Are Leaving Church ... and Rethinking Faith,* (Baker Books, 2011).

6. Theolographics, a term coined by George Barna, refers to the spiritual practices, beliefs and self-identification of individuals.

7. The Conference Board, "More Than Half of US Workers Are Satisfied with Their Jobs," September 1, 2017, https://www.conference-board.org/press/pressdetail.cfm ?pressid=7184.

8. Gallup, Inc., *State of the American Workplace* (Gallup, 2017).

9. Derek Thompson, "Who's Had the Worst Recession: Boomers, Millennials, or Gen-Xers?" *The Atlantic,* September 13, 2011, https://www.theatlantic.com/business/archive/2011/09/whos-had-the-worst-recession-boomers-millennials-or-gen-xers/245056/.

10. Business Wire, "Finally Feeling Better About Retirement, Optimistic Baby Boomers Offer Lessons for Younger Generations," September 25, 2017, https://www.businesswire .com/news/home/20170925005167/en/Finally-Feeling-Retirement-Optimistic-Baby-Boomers-Offer.

11. Pedro Nicolaci da Costa, "Millennial Graduates of the Great Recession Are Struggling to Make up Ground in One Key Area," *Business Insider,* July 27, 2017, http://www .pulselive.co.ke/bi/finance/finance-millennial-graduates-of-the-great-recession-are-struggling-to-make-up-ground-in-one-key-area-id7067147.html.

12. Travis M Andrews, "It's Official: Millennials Have Surpassed Baby Boomers to Become America's Largest Living Generation," *Washington Post,* April 26, 2016, https://www.washingtonpost.com/news/morning-mix/wp/2016/04/26/its-official-millennials-have-surpassed-baby-boomers-to-become-americas-largest-living-generation/?utm_term=.bbb050f2c4b1.

13. Albert Wolters, *Creation Regained: Biblical Basis for a Reformational Worldview* (Grand Rapids, MI: Eerdmans, 2005), 44.

14. Wolters, *Creation Regained,* 45.

15. Wolters, *Creation Regained,* 78-79.

16. Wolters, *Creation Regained,* 72.

17. Timothy Keller, *Every Good Endeavor: Connecting Your Work to God's Work* (New York: Penguin, 2012), 196.

18. Wolters, *Creation Regained,* 79.

19. Keller, *Every Good Endeavor,* 197.

20. Keller, *Every Good Endeavor.*

21. Keller, *Every Good Endeavor.*

22. Nikki Graf, Anna Brown and Eileen Patten, "The Narrowing, but Persistent, Gender Gap in Pay," Pew Research Center Website, April 9, 2018, http://www.pewresearch.org/fact-tank/2018/04/09/gender-pay-gap-facts/.

23. Pew Research Center, "Chapter 2: What Makes a Good Leader, and Does Gender Matter?" Pew Research Center Website, January 14, 2015, http://www.pewsocialtrends.org/2015/01/14/chapter-2-what-makes-a-good-leader-and-does-gender-matter/.

24. Anne Marie Slaughter, "Why Women Still Can't Have It All," *The Atlantic,* July / August 2012, https://www.theatlantic.com/magazine/archive/2012/07/why-women-still-cant-have-it-all/309020/.

25. Sarah Jane Glynn, "Breadwinning Mothers Are Increasingly the U.S. Norm," Center for American Progress website, December 19, 2016, https://www.americanprogress.org/issues/women/reports/2016/12/19/295203/breadwinning-mothers-are-increasingly-the-u-s-norm/.

26. Wendy Wang and Kim Parker, "Record Share of Americans Have Never Married," Pew Research Center website, September 24, 2014, http://www.pewsocialtrends.org/2014/09/24/record-share-of-americans-have-never-married/.

27. Frank Newport and Joy Wilke, "Desire for Children Still Norm in U.S.," Gallup, September 25, 2013, http://news.gallup.com/poll/164618/desire-children-norm.aspx.

28. Wang and Parker, "Record Share of Americans."

29. Danielle Paquette, "Working Dads Make More Money Than Working Moms in Every State," *Washington Post,* June 3, 2015, https://www.washingtonpost.com/news/wonk/wp/2015/06/03/working-dads-make-more-money-than-working-moms-in-every-state.

30. Promundo, *Helping Dads Care,* Promundo, 2018, https://promundoglobal.org/resources/helping-dads-care/.

31. Claire Cain Miller, "The Motherhood Penalty vs. the Fatherhood Bonus," *The Upshot* (blog), *New York Times,* September 6, 2014, https://www.nytimes.com/2014/09/07/upshot/a-child-helps-your-career-if-youre-a-man.html.

32. Natalie Kitroeff and Jessica Silver-Greenberg, "Pregnancy Discrimination Is Rampant Inside America's Biggest Companies," *New York Times,* June 15, 2018, https://www.nytimes.com/interactive/2018/06/15/business/pregnancy-discrimination.html.

33. Roni Caryn Rabin, "Put a Ring on It? Millennials Are in No Hurry," *New York Times,* May 29, 2018, https://www.nytimes.com/2018/05/29/well/mind/millennials-love-marriage-sex-relationships-dating.html.

34. J Stewart Bundeson and Jeffrey A Thompson, "The Call of the Wild: Zookeepers, Callings, and the Double-edged Sword of Deeply Meaningful Work," *Administrative Science Quarterly* 54, March 1, 2009, 32–57.

35. Alexis Krikovich et al., "Women in the Workplace 2017," McKinsey & Company website, October 2017, https://www.mckinsey.com/~/media/McKinsey/Global%20Themes/Gender%20Equality/Women%20in%20the%20Workplace%202017/Women-in-the-Workplace-2017-v2.ashx.

36. Andreas Schick and Richard H Steckel, "Height, Human Capital, and Earnings: The Contributions of Cognitive and Noncognitive Ability," *Journal of Human Capital* 9, no. 1 (Spring 2015) http://www.jstor.org/stable/10.1086/679675?seq=1#page_scan_tab_contents.

37. United States Department of Labor, Bureau of Labor Statistics, "Distribution of Employment by Wage Range for Each Major Occupational Group, 2017," Bureau of Labor Statistics website, https://www.bls.gov/oes/2017/may/distribution.htm.

38. United States Department of Labor, Bureau of Labor Statistics, "Data Tables for the Overview of May 2017 Occupational Employment and Wages," Bureau

of Labor Statistics website, https://www.bls.gov/oes/2017/may/featured_data.htm#largest2.

39. Mark Brush, "The Average Michigan Family Needs $52,330 a Year to 'Make Ends Meet,'" Michigan Radio website, http://michiganradio.org/post/average-michigan-family-needs-52330-year-make-ends-meet; Massachusetts Institute of Technology, "Living Wage Calculator," MIT website, http://livingwage.mit.edu/.

40. Barna Group, Spiritual Conversations in the Digital Age (Ventura, Ca.: Barna Group, 2018) 14.

41. Garber, Visions of Vocation.

42. Stephanie L Shackelford, "Career Calling in Emerging Adult Christian Females: A Narrative Analysis." Order No. 10745785 Northeastern University, 2018. Ann Arbor: ProQuest. Web. 26 June 2018.

43. Todd B Kashdan et al., "Curiosity Protects Against Interpersonal Agression: Cross-Sectional, Daily Process, and Behavioral Evidence," Journal of Personality 81, no. 1 (February 2013) https://onlinelibrary.wiley.com/doi/full/10.1111/j.1467-6494.2012.00783.x.

44. Dan M Kahan et al., "Science Curiosity and Political Information Processing," Political Psychology 38, no. S1 (February 2017) https://onlinelibrary.wiley.com/doi/full/10.1111/pops.12396.

45. Megan Price, "Change Through Curiosity in the Insight Approach to Conflict," Revista de Mediacion 11, 1, e3 (2018) https://revistademediacion.com/wp-content/uploads/2018/01/Revista21-en-e3.pdf.

46. Bryan J Dik and Ryan D Duffy, "Calling and Vocation at Work: Definitions and Prospects for Research and Practice," The Counseling Psychologist 37, no3 (2009) 424–450. doi: 10.1177/0011000008316430.

47. Shackelford, "Career Calling in Emerging Adult Christian Females."

48. Shackelford, "Career Calling in Emerging Adult Christian Females."

49. Shackelford, "Career Calling in Emerging Adult Christian Females."

50. Emma Seppala and Julia Moeller, "1 in 5 Highly Engaged Employees Is at Risk of Burnout," Harvard Business Review, February 2, 2018, https://hbr.org/2018/02/1-in-5-highly-engaged-employees-is-at-risk-of-burnout.

51. Susan Scutti, "Yes, Sitting Too Long Can Kill You, Even if You Exercise," CNN, September 12,2017, https://www.cnn.com/2017/09/11/health/sitting-increases-risk-of-death-study/index.html.

52. American Psychological Association, "How Stress Affects Your Health," APA website, http://www.apa.org/helpcenter/stress.aspx.

53. Ryan D Duffy et al., "Perceiving a Calling, Living a Calling, and Job Satisfaction: Testing a Moderated, Multiple Mediator Model," Journal of Counseling Psychology 59, no. 1 (2012) 50–59.

54. Maria K Pavlova and Rainer K Silbereisen, "Dispositional Optimism Fosters. Opportunity-Congruent Coping with Occupational Uncertainty," Journal of Personality 81, no.1 (February 2013) 76–86.

55. Mark Labberton, Called: The Crisis and Promise of Following Jesus Today, (Westmont, IL: IVP Books, 2014) 126.

56. Conducted among a nationally representative sample of 1,000 U.S. adults from May 10, 2013 to July 1, 2013

57. Based on telephone surveys with a nationally representative sample of 1,005 U.S. adults, conducted by Barna Group in July 2006.

58. Wendell Berry, "Two Economies," Review & Expositor 81, no. 2 (1984).

ACKNOWLEDGMENTS

Barna Group is incredibly grateful to Abilene Christian University, especially Dr. Phil Schubert, president, and Dr. Robert Rhodes, provost, for their support and endorsement in the commissioning of this project. We want to acknowledge the important role and contribution of Dr. Ben Ries, director of ACU's Center for Vocational Formation, who, along with Drs. Stephen Johnson and Carson Reed, collaborated with Barna on bringing *Christians at Work* to life. The project was guided early on by input from other academic leaders and faculty members, including Dr. Darryl Tippens, Dr. Brad Crisp, Dr. Suzie Macaluso and Dr. Monty Lynn.

This report's findings were strengthened by the insights of practitioners and thought leaders who contributed through qualitative interviews, Q&As, columns and more. That lengthy list includes: Sheryl Anderson, Dean Batali, Cory Maxwell-Coghlan, Woody Faulk, Makoto Fujimura, Phil Graves, Heather Grizzle, Bethany Jenkins, Scott Kauffmann, Pamela Ebstyne King, Michaela O'Donnell Long, David Martinez, Sheeba Philip, Jo Saxton, Jeff Shinabarger, Roxanne Stone, Darien M. Sykes and Sam Whitehawk.

The research for this study was coordinated by Brooke Hempell and Traci Hochmuth. Daniel Copeland assisted with data review. Bill Denzel helped inform the broader vision of this first Barna study committed to the topic of vocation. Stephanie Shackelford, whose research on the subject of calling so enriched Barna's own, conducted qualitative interviews. Under the editorial direction of Roxanne Stone, the writing team included Susan Mettes and Alyce Youngblood. Doug Brown proofread the manuscript. Annette Allen designed the cover, interior layout and data visualizations. Brenda Usery managed production. Jennifer Hamel coordinated as project manager. Additional thanks for the support of our Barna colleagues Amy Brands, Aly Hawkins, Pam Jacob, Savannah Kimberlin, David Kinnaman, Steve McBeth, Caitlin Schuman, Jess Villa and Todd White.

Many thanks to Dale and Tod Brown for generously making this project possible, for their ongoing partnership with Barna and with ACU and for their passion for developing and serving leaders in the Church.

ABOUT THE PROJECT PARTNERS

Barna Group is a research firm dedicated to providing actionable insights on faith and culture, with a particular focus on the Christian Church. Since 1984, Barna has conducted more than one million interviews in the course of hundreds of studies, and has become a go-to source for organizations that want to better understand a complex and changing world from a faith perspective.

Barna's clients and partners include a broad range of academic institutions, churches, non-profits and businesses, such as Alpha, the Templeton Foundation, Fuller Seminary, the Bill and Melinda Gates Foundation, Maclellan Foundation, DreamWorks Animation, Focus Features, Habitat for Humanity, The Navigators, NBC-Universal, the ONE Campaign, Paramount Pictures, the Salvation Army, Walden Media, Sony and World Vision. The firm's studies are frequently quoted by major media outlets such as *The Economist*, BBC, CNN, *USA Today*, the *Wall Street Journal*, Fox News, *Huffington Post*, *The New York Times* and the *Los Angeles Times*.

WWW.BARNA.COM

Abilene Christian University has been educating Christ-centered global leaders since 1906. The university offers 77 baccalaureate majors that include more than 135 areas of study, 30 master's degree and three doctoral programs. ACU Dallas, a branch campus in Addison, is the home of the university's online graduate and professional programs. The university enrolls about 5,000 students, generally from 51 states and territories and 40 nations, and has about 90,000 alumni in more than 100 nations. Its graduates are best-selling authors; winners of the Pulitzer Prize, Olympic medals, and Emmy, Grammy, Telly and Dove awards; and national leaders in education, business, law, science and medicine, journalism, psychology and ministry.

WWW.ACU.EDU

Barna

Stay Informed About Cultural Trends

Spiritual Conversations in the Digital Age
Technology is just one of the forces that has altered evangelism. Learn how these changes have opened new avenues to reach and engage the lost.

Gen Z
Critical data to help the church effectively reach, serve and equip the emerging generation to confidently follow Jesus in today's post-Christian context

The State of Pastors
Pastoring in a complex cultural moment is not easy. Read about how church leaders are holding up in this whole-life assessment of U.S. pastors.

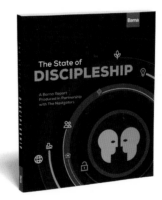

The State of Discipleship
In an era when spiritual growth is increasingly self-directed, if not neglected altogether, how effective are discipleship programs? Learn from leaders whose churches exemplify excellence in discipleship.

What Can Barna Do For You?

Barna

When you need to make a decision, you want good information to guide you. You want a trusted advisor who knows the times. For more than 30 years, Barna has been providing reliable data and actionable insights to the leaders of some of the most influential organizations of our day. Whatever decision you're trying to make, Barna can help.

Custom Research
Accurate, timely, and affordable research for organizations, faith leaders, entrepreneurs and innovators

Barna Polls
Shared-cost research that provides strategic insights about pastors or U.S. adults at minimal cost

Consulting
Actionable recommendations for your organization, grounded in research and an understanding of your context

Resources
Published research and insights for leaders and decision makers

Learn more about Barna's work at barna.com/services

Discover
Listening to understand your unique needs and expectations

Design
Determining the best questions and methodology to ensure meaningful and reliable findings

Gather
Ensuring that the data is accurate and representative of your key audiences

Analyze
Interpreting results and identifying key patterns, trends and insights

Deliver
Creating custom monographs, reports or presentations to fit your needs

Advise
Applying Barna's decades of knowledge and experience to give you confidence to take action